A1SB

An A1 Sporting Books publication
in association with NMG Publishing
© Terry Baker/Norman Giller/Michael Giller 2010

First published in 2010 by A1 Sporting Books
Unit 20, 12 Airfield Road, Christchurch, Dorset. BH23 3TQ.

A CIP catalogue for this title is available from the British Library
ISBN 978-0-9543243-3-9
Typeset and designed by NMG Publishing, Dorset, UK
Printed and bound in the United Kingdom by Antony Rowe Limited
Bumper's Farm, Chippenham, Wiltshire SN14 6LH

The majority of photographs in this book have been provided by premier promotions agency A1 Sporting Speakers (www.a1sportingspeakers.com). Best efforts have been made to clear all copyrights. The Art Turner illustrations are ©Art Turner 2010

The Publisher and authors give special thanks for their efficiency and friendly co-operation to the Antony Rowe team, and in particular to Chris Jones, Mark Radley, Geoff Fisher and claret-and-blue-blooded Hammer Dave Biggs

HAMMERS '80

Revisiting a West Ham season to remember

NORMAN GILLER and TERRY BAKER

Introduced by

SIR TREVOR BROOKING

Edited by Michael Giller

Illustrations: Art Turner

A1SB

Dedicated to the memories of
John Lyall and **Ron Greenwood**
West Ham managers supreme and
gentlemen of the first order

Art Turner
2010

HAMMERS '80: Contents

Sir Trevor Brooking, a great ambassador for football in general and West Ham in particular

IT is quite unbelievable that thirty years have gone by since West Ham won the FA Cup at Wembley in 1980. The match against Arsenal was one of the most memorable of my career, and rarely a week goes by without somebody mentioning my winning goal, one of just a handful of headers that I scored in more than 600 games for the Hammers.

I cannot claim that it was a stunning Alan Shearer-style power header, but the fact that it found the net and won the Cup for us made it, for me, a goal in a million. We remain the last team outside the top division to have captured the FA Cup, and to this day I don't think some Arsenal fans have got over the shock of the defeat.

It is easy to get emotional thinking back on that remarkable season. John Lyall, our manager and a true gentleman of football, is no longer with us, and I am glad to know that this book has been dedicated to the memories of both John and his predecessor Ron Greenwood, two men who had a huge influence on my career.

You are in good hands with sports historian Norman Giller telling the story of the season. He was right at the heart of things as a respected reporter, who was ghosting columns during the run up to the Wembley final for both Billy Bonds and Pat Rice, the rival captains.

Publisher and co-author Terry Baker is a Dorset-based entrepreneur who specialises in the sports nostalgia market. He represents an impressive array of sporting legends such as Jimmy Greaves, Sir Geoff Hurst, Sir Henry Cooper and has worked closely with Pelé and Maradona.

Terry's publishing company, A1 Sporting Books, plans a series of sports nostalgia publications, and I am delighted to recommend this revisiting of the 1979-80 season which, for West Ham fans and players, grew into something very special.

Michael Giller, Norman's West Ham-born son, is a leading sports statistician, whose stats give a fascinating lift to the facts, and the illustrations by former Fleet Street graphics master Art Tuner are of the highest quality.

For those of you who were there, this will be a nostalgic and at times moving trip down memory lane. For the younger generation it will serve as a history lesson on the esteem in which West Ham were held, playing First Division football from a Second Division base, long before the days of the Premier League.

Fasten your safety belts ready for a journey back into the past before the days of the full foreign invasion, and in a season when West Ham dreams were not fading and their fortunes not hiding. Enjoy the ride.

A Class Act by TERRY BAKER

MY publishing company A1 Sporting Books specialises in the nostalgia market, and we know from the many enquiries we get that there is a lot of interest in the remarkable FA Cup final of 1980, when West Ham shocked mighty Arsenal to defeat. Thirty years on they remain the last team from outside the top division to have won the most prestigious of all domestic cup competitions.

It was a fascinating and at times frantic period in our football, bridging the old world and the new. The season before, Tottenham had started a face-changing revolution by bringing in overseas players when they made a double swoop for Argentinian World Cup stars Osvaldo Ardiles and Ricky Villa. West Ham's FA Cup final team consisted of ten Englishmen and a Scot. Can you imagine that happening today?

I called in Team Giller – prolific author Norman and his statistician son, Michael – to help me tell the story of one of the most amazing FA Cup feats in history. Norman has all the right qualifications to give an in-depth report on West Ham. He is a former sports editor of the local West Ham newspaper, was chief *Daily Express* football reporter when the Hammers were enjoyng the best days in their history, and he reported the Final sitting in the ITV gantry at Wembley alongside his close friend and exceptional commentator, Brian Moore. During the build-up to the Final he was welcome in both camps, ghosting newspaper columns for the skippers Pat Rice of the Arsenal and West Ham's Billy Bonds.

You could have got 50-1 on West Ham winning the Cup at the start of the season. The usual suspects – Manchester United, Liverpool and Arsenal – were the short-price favourites. Hammers were regrouping after coming out of the golden era at Upton Park of Moore, Hurst and Peters.

West Ham may have been in the Second Division that season, but they were making the purists purr with the quality of their football. In skipper Bonds they had a player with the heart of a lion and insatiable energy and enthusiasm, while Trevor Brooking – then celebrating fifteen years as a professional with the Hammers – was playing to his peak, taking defences apart with his clever dribbling and measured passes. Uh, but he was not troubling defences with his heading!

I am delighted that Sir Trevor has supported this book with an introduction and – if you are one of the lucky ones – with his prized autograph. English football has rarely had a finer ambassador, honoured with a knighthood for his services to the game that he

Sir Trevor Brooking during a signing session at Terry Baker's A1 Sporting Speakers headquarters

has always graced with dignity and sportsmanship. He is the Director of Football for the Football Association, and remains one of the most respected voices in the business.

As will become evident in the following pages, his contribution to West Ham's triumph was much more than the winning goal he scored in the Final. His midfield scheming partnership with Alan Devonshire was as creative a tandem team as there was in the country, and it made no sense that they were down in the Second Division.

West Ham have always had a proud tradition of being a footballing side, and in that 1979-80 season there were many who considered they were playing more precise and better-planned football than many of the major teams in the First Division.

While concentrating on the FA Cup, they were also trying to play their way back up to the top table. Many critics said they would only get promotion if they started playing a more physical game. When manager John Lyall was asked why his team did not kick back when kicked, he said: "That is not the West Ham way. If we are going to win anything this season it will be by playing football, pure and simple."

That is why West Ham are always that little bit special, even when things are not going right. As they proved with their FA Cup run in 1980, they are – like Sir Trevor – a class act. This book provides all the necessary evidence.

Tony Baker

Under the Greenwood Tree by Norman Giller

So that you feel comfortable with me writing this book, let me lay out my qualifications. Then you can relax in the knowledge that between us, Terry Baker and I will be bringing you the best possible reconstruction of that remarkable 1979-80 season that culminated with West Ham lifting the FA Cup for the third (and most unlikely) time.

For starters I am an East Londoner, and my two children were both born in the same Stratford hospital in the 1960s as a boxer by the name of Lennox Lewis.

I was Sports Editor of the local newspaper, the *Stratford Express*, back when Ted Fenton was manager, Noel Cantwell the captain, 'Dick and the Duchess' (John Dick and Malcolm Musgrove) were left-wing partners, John 'Muffin the Mule' Bond at right-back, and a young blond boy from Barking called Bobby Moore was about to make his professional debut.

Goalkeeping hero Ernie Gregory lived in the next street, and another near neighbour and close friend was legendary scout Wally St Pier, who deserves a place in the West Ham hall of fame for the number of young stars he discovered.

In the same season that I started out as a young reporter on the *Stratford Express* West Ham won promotion as champions of the Second Division, and our paper was instrumental in launching the first Hammer of the Year vote, which continues to this day. Andy Malcolm was the first winner, and we gave a special award to Malcolm Allison, who was forced to give up football after contracting tuberculosis. The young Mooro took over his number six shirt, and he and I became life-long buddies.

Also on the West Ham groundstaff was an enthusiastic full-back by the name of John Lyall, an always-smiling and friendly lad from Ilford. I was with him at the best and worst moments of his life.

The worst was when he was told that his succession of knee injuries meant that he had to give up his playing career. He was just twenty-two. John took it on the chin, and made up his mind that if he couldn't play he would teach others how to do it. The right way. The West Ham way.

His best moment was at Wembley on May 10 1980 when, against all the odds, he lifted the FA Cup for the second time as West Ham manager. These were the sort of

Ron Greenwood, who was the thinking man's manager

precious moments he had dreamt about ever since his playing career had been cruelly cut short twenty years earlier.

While John was off on his coaching courses in the early 1960s, my career took me to Fleet Street, first to the *Daily Herald* and then to the *Daily Express*, where I became chief football reporter in the same year that England won the World Cup with huge Claret and Blue influence.

The key moment for West Ham was when Ron Greenwood arrived to take over from Ted Fenton as manager in 1961. A one-time cultured centre-half with Brentford, Chelsea and Fulham, Ron was a thinking man's manager.

He had been making a name for himself as Arsenal coach and a disciple of England manager Walter Winterbottom, the 'Father' of modern British coaching techniques. He brought all his fresh thinking and new tactical theories to Upton Park, feeding them into youngsters like Bobby Moore, Geoff Hurst and Martin Peters.

We will relive some of Greenwood's glory moments with the Hammers at the back of this book, but our focus will first be on when he handed over the managerial reins to his right-hand man John Lyall.

We used to joke, John and I, that we had both grown up under the Greenwood Tree. As a young reporter, I discovered all about the intricacies of modern football from

Greenwood, listening and learning from a man who devoted every spare second to studying the international football developments. We got so close that he allowed me the privilege of carrying the FA Cup on a London tube train!

It was the Monday after the victory over Preston in 1964 and I had been driving him to a press conference in the West End. We got locked in a monster traffic jam and abandoned the car at Mile End, continuing the journey on the Central Line, with me holding the precious FA Cup in a large zip-up bag. The *Daily Express* ran a huge picture the next day with the caption: "Ron Greenwood takes the FA Cup on the tube, accompanied by a minder ..." I was that minder, on the *Daily Herald* at the time. Within a month I had been signed by the *Express*, impressed by the way I had become Greenwood's close confidant.

Meanwhile, John Lyall had willingly become Ron's apprentice and West Ham manager in waiting. He idolized Greenwood, and sucked in all the knowledge he could from him and then added creative ideas of his own. It all came together in a wonderful footballing cocktail in that 1979-80 season.

I wish there was a happy ending to this Master and Apprentice story. Sadly it ended in tears when Greenwood and Lyall died within weeks and just a few miles of each other down in Suffolk in 2006.

Between them, they had given West Ham the greatest moments in the club's history, and Terry Baker and I were in total agreement that it would be fitting to dedicate this book to their memories.

The build-up to the 1979-80 FA Cup final was a particularly busy and rewarding time for me. I ghosted columns in the London *Evening News* for rival FA Cup final captains Billy Bonds and Pat Rice, and I watched the match from the ITV gantry at Wembley alongside my close pal Brian Moore, the Voice of Football. I remember him being distraught because he called the winning goal for Stuart Pearson. Like thousands of others at Wembley that day, he did not see Trevor Brooking going down on his knees to head-flick the ball into the net after Pearson had mis-hit his shot. It is all coming back to me now like a wonderful dream.

Hopefully you now accept that I am qualified to write the background story to that glorious 1979-80 season for the Hammers.

First of all, let's meet the cast ...

THE WEST HAM SQUAD 1979-80

Player	Born	Ht/Wt	Previous club
Phil Parkes	Aug 8 1950, Sedgley, Staffs	6ft 3in 14-13	QPR
Ray Stewart	Sep 7, 1959, Stanley, Perthshire	5ft 10in 12-0	Dundee United
Frank Lampard	Sep 20 1948, East Ham	5ft 11in 12-9	West Ham Youth
Billy Bonds	Sep 17 1946, Woolwich	6ft 0in 13-4	Charlton
Alvin Martin	July 29 1958, Bootle	6ft 1in 13-0	West Ham Youth
Alan Devonshire	Apr 13 1956, Park Royal	5ft 10.5in 11-0	Southall
Paul Allen	Aug 28 1962, Aveley, Essex	5ft 7in 9-12	West Ham Youth
Stuart Pearson	June 21 1949, Hull	5ft 8.5in 11-12	Man United
David Cross	Dec 8 1950, Heywood, Lancs	6ft 1in 12-2	West Brom
Trevor Brooking	Oct 2 1948, Barking	6ft 0.5in 13-0	West Ham Youth
Geoff Pike	Sep 28 1956, Clapton	5ft 7in 11-3	West Ham Youth
Paul Brush	Feb 22 1958, Plaistow	5ft 11in 11-12	West Ham Youth
Pat Holland	Sep 13 1950, Poplar	5ft 10in 11-7	West Ham Youth
Jimmy Neighbour	Nov 15 1950, Chingford	5ft 7.5in 10-8	Norwich City
Billy Lansdowne	Apr 28 1959, Epping	6ft 0in 11-6	West Ham Youth
Nicky Morgan	Oct 30 1959, East Ham	5ft 10in 12-8	West Ham Youth

These were the sixteen players that manager John Lyall called on at least six times during the 1979-80 Second Division season when West Ham made a bold bid for promotion, but finally finished seventh. There were also brief appearances by Dale Banton and Mark Smith, with veteran goalkeeper Bobby Ferguson twice filling in for Phil Parkes.

Six players appeared in all eight FA Cup matches, including the Final – Phil Parkes, Ray Stewart, Alan Devonshire, Stuart Pearson. Paul Allen and Geoff Pike – Allen and Pike including one substitute appearance each for the injured Pearson. Frank Lampard, Alvin Martin and Trevor Brooking played in seven of the ties, including the Final. John Lyall called on fifteen players in total on the road to Wembley.

Born: Sedgley, Staffs
August 8 1950

Position: Goalkeeper
Ht 6ft 3in Wt 14st 13lbs
League games:
Walsall (1968-70) 52;
QPR (1970-79) 344;
West Ham (1979-90) 344;
Ipswich (1990-91) 3.
Total: 743

1 England cap
(v Portugal 1974)

A CARPENTER by trade, it often seemed big Phil had built a wooden wall across his goal. He was a magnificent goalkeeper who would have won a shelf-full of England caps but for being around at the same time as England goalkeeping legends Gordon Banks, Peter Shilton and Ray Clemence.

He cost West Ham a then world record £565,000 when John Lyall brought him to Upton Park from Queens Park Rangers in 1979. Dave Sexton, his previous manager at Rangers, had tried several times to take him to Manchester United, but it was the size of the bold Hammers bid that persuaded QPR to finally let him go.

Phil took over in the West Ham goal from Scottish international Bobby Ferguson, who himself had cost a then world record £65,000 when bought from Kilmarnock by Ron Greenwood in 1967.

Built like one of the wardrobes he now makes for a living, the 6ft 3in, 15-stone Parkes was surprisingly mobile for such a hefty man and could move with lightning speed between his posts. He had good positional sense, large, safe hands and the reflexes of a quick-on-the-draw wild west gunman. Phil was also as brave as they come in an era when forwards could still lay into goalkeepers without risking being sent to the Tower.

Mind you, it was a foolish forward who took him on in a shoulder-to-shoulder duel, and it was a common sight to see opponents bouncing off him at set pieces.

Big Phil slipped comfortably into a West Ham defence that had been giving away goals like a registered charity, and he quickly got an understanding with central defenders Billy Bonds and, in particular, Alvin Martin. They knew almost instinctively which position to take up and when to accept responsibility for a cross.

In all, Phil played 444 games for the Hammers. The highlights were the FA Cup win at the end of his first year, helping them back to the First Division in his second full season and to the League Cup final against Liverpool in the same year. And he was still the defiant last line of defence when the Irons finished in their best-ever third place in the old First Division in 1988. This was not his personal highest place in the top table.

Graphics artist Art Turner captures West Ham goalkeeping legend Phil Parkes then and now

He had helped QPR finish second under Dave Sexton in their most successful season of 1975-76. His skipper at QPR was Frank McLintock, who had led Arsenal to the League and Cup double in 1970-71. "I was lucky to play with outstanding goalkeepers like Gordon Banks at Leicester and Bob Wilson at Arsenal," said Frank. "Phil was in their class, and it was always comforting for me to turn round and see him standing on the line like a church steeple. Phil was big but never ever clumsy. He was brilliant at set pieces, happy to take charge of his territory and accepting full responsibility for going for the awkward crosses. He had a magnificent career at Rangers, and then played every bit as well when he moved across London to West Ham. The astonishing thing is that he won only one England cap. Had he been born across the border in Scotland he would have had been a regular at the back of Scotland's defence. Phil was particularly good with his distribution, and for both Rangers and the Hammers he started many counter-attacks with an accurately thrown ball."

A committed competitor on the pitch, Phil was the proverbial gentle giant off, quietly spoken with an easy smile and a sharp sense of Black Country humour. He was an excellent team player and good for team spirit whenever the going got tough.

He famously got the hump only once. Phil had collected his one England cap against Portugal in 1974, and was continually called up into Don Revie's squads without being picked for the game.

In 1976 he was selected for the match against Wales, and this time Revie promised him the second-half of the match. With the score at 0-0 at half-time and Phil gloved up and ready to go, the England boss changed his mind and told Ray Clemence to continue. From then on, peeved Phil preferred not to be considered for international duty. Today, he would walk into the England team, and his huge presence would have spread confidence throughout the side.

In a 2003 poll for West Ham's greatest goalkeeper, Phil beat Ludek Miklosko to the No 1 jersey. Witnesses of his performance against West Brom right at the start of the 1980 FA Cup run described it as the finest goalkeeping display they had ever seen.

> ## QUOTE UNQUOTE: Phil Parkes
> 'I have no regrets about my career, even though I didn't collect many medals. I loved every minute of it, particularly the rapport I had with the fans both at Loftus Road and Upton Park. In Dave Sexton and then lovely John Lyall I played under two of the nicest managers in the game. Two things I would liked to have had from today's game – the money and the pitches. We used to play on some shockers, and you rarely got a true bounce that you could trust. The Cup run to Wembley in 1980 was the highlight.'

DEADEYE Ray Stewart is chiefly remembered at Upton Park for 1) being a 'foreigner', and 2) having the most accurate penalty kick in the game.

Remarkably, the proud Scot was the only non-Englishman to play in any of the West Ham FA Cup-winning teams of 1964, 1975 and 1980.

He arrived at the Boleyn Ground for £430,000 in 1979 carrying the tag of the most expensive teenage footballer in the British game, and he spent the next twelve years proving that it was money well spent.

Ray was as tough as Aberdeen granite, and the West Ham fans quickly nicknamed him 'Tonka' after the indestructible toy.

He came into football while it was still a game of physical contact, and had a mean and solid tackle that disheartened a string of wingers. Following in the footsteps of such dependable right-backs as John Bond, Joe Kirkup and John McDowell, Ray proved their equal in his consistency and calmness under pressure. If he came up against a winger who was skinning him, he was not shy in delivering his opponent to the Chicken Run supporters.

On the many occasions when he was asked to play in midfield, he proved himself a reliable anchorman, winning the ball and then passing it as quickly as possible to his more creative midfield partners.

He has gone down into West Ham legend for his shooting accuracy from the penalty spot. Ray netted 76 of 86 penalties, although he disputes that stat and claims to have missed only five times.

Asked the secret of his success with the 12-yard challenge, Ray advised: "Shoot hard, shoot straight, don't try to be too clever and don't think too much about it."

There was a simple reason for Ray's high scoring ratio: practice, practice, practice. He used to always prolong his training so that he could add penalty-taking time. Ray used cones as his targets rather than having a goalkeeper on the line. He was interested only in placement and by not having to give thought to a goalie's movement could concentrate solely on accuracy.

> **Born: Stanley, Perthshire September 7 1959**
> **Ht 5ft 10in Wt 12st**
> **Position: Right-back**
> **League games:**
> **Dundee United (1976-79)**
> **44 (5 goals)**
> **West Ham (1979-91)**
> **345 (62 goals)**
> **St Johnstone (1991-92)**
> **17 (3 goals)**
> **Stirling Albion (1994-95) 2**
> **Total:**
> **408 games, 70 goals**
> **10 Scotland caps, 1 goal (1981-87)**

Ray Stewart, a deadeye finisher from the penalty spot

Famous for his power from the spot, he cleverly changed his tactics when he considered it necessary. In the 1981 League Cup final against Liverpool he kidded goalkeeper Ray Clemence into thinking he was going to produce his usual piledriver, and as the England goalkeeper threw himself one way Ray calmly rolled the ball into the opposite side of the net. It was coolness personified.

His most memorable penalty was against Aston Villa on the way to Wembley in 1980, which will feature in our special reports section later in our book. He was second highest scorer in the 1979-80 season, with ten goals in the League, three in the FA Cup and one in the League Cup. Ten of his 14 goals came from the penalty spot.

Ray's biggest honour was to represent his country, and he was inconsolable when Jock Stein made him one of the players chopped at the last minute from his 1982 World Cup squad for the finals in Spain.

"It was always my dream to play for Scotland in a World Cup finals," he said at the time. "Being left out when so close is just heart breaking, particularly as I had made it into the squad of 24, with just two to lose out. I had played in the midweek win against Northern Ireland and on the eve of the Home Championship match against England Jock Stein called us together and announced bluntly: 'It's easier to tell the lads who are not going to the finals. Tommy Burns and Ray Stewart, you are staying behind.' It was like a public execution and my lowest moment in football."

Ray had the character to overcome his disappointment, and played a prominent role in the season that the Hammers finished third in the First Division title race. In 1981-82 he was one of the League's leading marksmen with thirteen goals – all from the penalty spot!

He returned home to Scotland in 1991 to wind down his career with St Johnstone and then Stirling Albion before trying his hand at management.

Whenever he returns to Upton Park, he is given the hero's welcome that he deserves.

QUOTE UNQUOTE: Ray Stewart

'I will always have some claret and blue inside me to go with the tartan blood. I was made to feel at home from the first minute I arrived at Upton Park, and it was wonderful to win the FA Cup at the end of my first season. It was particularly satisfying for our manager John Lyall, who had taken a chance on a young Scottish lad by paying out what was then a huge amount of money. The West Ham fans made me feel like an honorary Cockney, and we had some great times together, and even when things were not going right they got behind the team and let us know they were there.'

**Born: East Ham
September 20 1948**

**Position: Left-back
Ht 5ft 11in, Wt 12st 9lbs
League games:
West Ham (1967-85)
551, 18 goals;
Southend United
(1985-86) 33, 1 goal
Total: 584, 19 goals
(Played 660 matches in
all for West Ham)**

2 England caps

THESE days Frank Lampard Senior usually only finds himself mentioned on the sports pages as the father of Frank Lampard Junior, magnificent midfielder who followed in his Dad's footsteps at Upton Park before finding fame and fortune with Chelsea and England.

Frank the First was a superb player in his own right, equally effective at right-back or left-back and a Hammers servant across 660 games and later assistant manager at the Boleyn ground to his brother-in-law Harry Redknapp. They were apprentice professionals together at West Ham and they married sisters, Pat and Sandra. It was the start of a dynasty, with Harry and Sandra producing son Jamie and Frank and Pat launching Frank junior into one of the outstanding modern football careers.

Ron Greenwood gave Lamps Senior his first-team debut for West Ham in November 1967, and he quickly established himself in his preferred left-back position alongside his idol Bobby Moore. Frank was a quick, athletic defender who got a master class in positional play from Mooro – "the greatest defender in the world," he has said time and again. His tackling was firm but fair, and he was expert at jockeying opponents into cul de sacs. Quick on the overlap, he used to link up neatly with Alan Devonshire as they moved into the opposition territory playing one-twos. He had a fair eye for goal and scored 24 career goals for the Hammers, about par for Frank Junior in a season! Unusually, he was a left-back who favoured his right foot.

Frank Senior, East Ham born and bred, is as pleasant a person as you could hope to meet. His wide, friendly bearded face is often wreathed with a smile, and he is an unassuming man without side or bitterness. He takes you as he finds you, and does not hog conversation and treats allcomers with respect. As you would expect, he is totally engrossed in the tactics and finer points of a game he played better than most.

His grasp of modern tactics caught the eye of England manager Sir Alf Ramsey, who selected him four times for the England Under-23 team before promoting him to the senior side against Yugoslavia in 1972. He partnered Mick Mills, also making his debut, in an experimental pairing, and they were unlucky to make their bow against

Frank Lampard Senior, a full-back of class and commitment

an exceptional Yugoslav winger called Dragan Dzajic. Ask anybody who knows their international football history and they will confirm that Dzajic was a player in the George Best class and style. He continually switched wings against England and gave both Mills and Lampard baptisms of fire in a 1-1 draw at Wembley.

Frank had to wait eight years for his next international call, by which time Ron Greenwood, the man who had first signed him for West Ham, was in charge of the England team. He awarded Lamps one cap in far-off Australia. England won the game to mark Australia's centenary of football 2-1, just eleven days after Frank had helped West Ham lift the FA Cup at Wembley. He and Frank Junior were the last father and son to win England caps.

Two serious injuries – a broken leg and a torn stomach muscle – severely hampered his career, otherwise he would definitely have topped 700 games with the Irons. He and Billy Bonds and Trevor Brooking were the only three survivors in the 1980 team from the side that won the FA Cup against Fulham in 1975.

As reward for his long service at Upton Park, he was allowed a free transfer in 1985, signing for Southend United, where Hammers legend and his big buddy, Bobby Moore, was in charge. He played 38 matches for The Shrimpers before hanging up his boots to concentrate on coaching.

Priority was given to helping his ten-year-old son Frank Junior – born in 1978 – learn the footballing basics, and by the time he signed for his Dad's old club he was already one of the outstanding young players in the country. Frank and his wife Pat – sadly, no longer with us – saw to it that Frank Junior not only got his feet educated but also his mind, and they sent him to the quality Brentwood school in Essex. It definitely paid off because Lamps Junior recently got a 'genius' rating in an IQ exam set at Chelsea.

When Harry Redknapp took over as Hammers manager in 1994 he brought in Frank Senior as his assistant, and they worked closely together until both were dismissed in 2001 – the same year that Frank Junior moved on to Chelsea. Lampard Pere was, without doubt, one of the finest defenders ever to pull on the claret and blue jersey.

QUOTE UNQUOTE: Frank Lampard Snr

'I was lucky to play my football at West Ham, where Ron Greenwood and John Lyall taught only good habits. When you think my earliest influences were the likes of Mooro, Martin Peters and Geoff Hurst then that can only rub off on you. I am obviously as proud as punch of the way my son's career has developed. I taught him the basics that I learnt at West Ham, that is a good worth ethic, discipline and attention to technique and passing accuracy. He has built on that foundation, and is twice the player I was.'

BUCCANEERING Billy Bonds was the heart of the Hammers throughout 27 years service to the club, playing like two men and bringing his atomic energy to every game in which he appeared.

He played with fire at right-back, ran his socks off in midfield and then answered manager Ron Greenwood's challenge to ride shotgun at the centre of the defence alongside Tommy Taylor.

A myth has grown that Billy was born to play for the Irons. In actual fact he had to cross the water to take over as the Hammers talisman.

He is a South Londoner, who started his career with his local club Charlton Athletic. Ron Greenwood was quick to spot his potential and brought him to Upton Park for a bargain fee of £50,000 in May 1967 after Billy had played 95 games for the Addicks.

It was the raw power of Bonzo allied to the silky skills of Trevor Brooking and Alan Devonshire that gave the 1979-80 Irons a dynamic mix that lifted them into the high-class category. Pros in the game smiled quietly to themselves when media critics often accused them of being 'Southern Softies.' Those who had felt the weight of a Bonds challenge would confirm that he was every bit as hard as a Nobby Stiles, a 'Bites Yer Legs' Hunter or a Tommy 'The Anfield Iron' Smith. Referees were continually on his case, and he was on nodding terms with the members of the FA disciplinary committee.

Billy seemed a permanent force after establishing himself in the team, and he played 124 consecutive League games until injury ended his run in October 1970.

After the departure of Bobby Moore to Craven Cottage in March 1974, Bonds was appointed to the captaincy and proved a natural leader who inspired by example. He led the club to an FA Cup final victory over the Moore/Mullery motivated Fulham in 1975 and to the final of the 1976 European Cup Winners' Cup despite a painful groin injury.

To save Billy from wear and tear, Greenwood switched him from his midfield marauding role to the back four in harness with Tommy Taylor. He continued to be

Born: Woolwich September 17 1946 Ht 6ft. Wt 13st 4lbs

Position: Defender/midfield

League games: Charlton Athletic (1964-67) 95 (1 goal) West Ham (1967-88) 663 (48 goals) Total: 758 games, 49 goals

2 England Under-23 caps

Buccaneering Billy Bonds, West Ham's Man for All Seasons

a huge influence on the team, now pushing forward from the back and demanding Bonds-style energy and enthusiasm from the players around him.

He was capped twice at England Under-23 international level but the nearest he got to a full cap was a place on the substitute's bench for a World Cup qualifying match against Italy in November 1977. Billy looked all set to break into the full England team when his old mentor Ron Greenwood shortlisted him for the match against Brazil in May 1981, but that plan was wrecked when he broke two ribs in a collision with the man mountain that is Phil Parkes.

His appearances record for West Ham – considering his near-100 games for Charlton before he arrived at Upton Park – is phenomenal. He played 663 League games for the Irons in a stretch of 21 years, despite losing a season and a half to injuries and did not give up until he was nearly 42. His final total of League and Cup games was 793.

He was honoured with an MBE in 1988, and in the same year got the recognition he deserved from his admiring fellow professionals when he was presented with the prestigious PFA Merit Award.

Bonzo captained the Hammers from 1974 to 1984, and continued to serve the club after his retirement. John Lyall put him in charge of the youth team, and he was later given the manager's job following the resignation of Lou Macari in the 1990 winter of discontent. They were the Yo-Yo years at the Boleyn as Billy took the club up, then down and then back up again to the First Division in successive seasons.

His 27 years with the Hammers ended under a cloud when he resigned in 1994 after he claimed the Board were kicking him upstairs to make way for Harry Redknapp to take over as manager. Bonzo may have gone, but his legend at Upton Park will never ever die. He was West Ham's Man for All Seasons. Billy's bubble never burst.

QUOTE UNQUOTE: Billy Bonds

'Under Ron Greenwood and then John Lyall, we always had the right attitude. No one was ever flash, and that included footballing greats like Bobby Moore, Geoff Hurst and Martin Peters. I only ever fell out with one player at West Ham. That was Ted MacDougall. We kept it under wraps, but I had a punch-up with him in the bath at Leeds. He was disrespectful to people. I didn't like that. It was not the West Ham way. The highlights for me, of course, had to be the FA Cup victories of 1975 and 1980. I am very proud of the fact that I am the only West Ham captain to have lifted the FA Cup twice. Even the great Mooro didn't manage that. I don't begrudge the professionals the money they earn today, but I do get annoyed when I see players picking up thirty grand a week who cannot control the ball properly. That is disgraceful.'

Born: Bootle
July 29, 1958

Position: Centre-half
Ht 6ft 1in Wt 13st

League games:
West Ham (1977-96)
469, 27 goals;
Leyton Orient (1996-97)
17 games
Total: 486, 27 goals

17 England caps
(1981-86)

IF Billy Bonds was the heart then Alvin Martin was the rock on which West Ham's success was built. He stood rock-solid in the middle of the West Ham defence, with the Ambling Alp Phil Parkes protecting his back and Bonzo playing like a lion alongside him.

It was not supposed to be like that for Alvin. In his boyhood dreams he used to lift the FA Cup for Everton, the club with which he started out on his football adventure in the 1970s.

The boy from Bootle was heartbroken when Everton declined to give him a full apprenticeship, and his ambition to become a professional took him for back-to-back trials with Queens Park Rangers and West Ham.

Ron Greenwood was instantly impressed and offered him a place as a Hammers apprentice. It was the start of a 20-year stay at Upton Park, where Alvin became part of the furniture.

Armed with a sharp Merseyside wit, he held his own with the Boleyn Cockneys and was liked by all. Team-mate Keith Robson gave him the nickname Stretch, that stuck because of the way he continually stretched his long legs to rob forwards of the ball.

He played a total of 586 games for the Irons, and collected 17 England caps between 1981 and 1986. His long-playing service to the Hammers was so appreciated that he shared with his partner – Billy Bonds – the honour of being the only two players granted two testimonial matches.

Bonds and Martin went together like bacon and eggs, and the sauce was provided by goalkeeper Phil Parkes. The three of them had a great understanding that brought stability and strength to the Hammers back line that had been frustratingly brittle before they got their act together.

In his formative days at Upton Park, Alvin was able to get a close up view of Bobby Moore. He remains gushing in his praise of The Master: "Bobby was the pinnacle of everything, the one man all the other players looked up to. He personified all that was good about the club. He had grace, mobility, humility and a fantastic technical ability as well as sportsmanship, and all these attributes were drilled into us from an early age."

Alvin Martin, the rock of ages for West Ham

The one area where he was superior to his idol Bobby was in the air. Alvin was fiercely competitive in challenging for high crosses, and often trespassed in the opposition penalty area to head vital goals.

He remains warmly appreciative of all that he learned about the game from Ron Greenwood and John Lyall, and with the eloquence that has taken him into a new career as a radio sports broadcaster he says: "They taught us not only how to play the game in the right spirit but how to live our lives. They encouraged us to believe that the game was more important than anything else. We knew winning was important, of course, but we always tried to put the playing of the game first. Ron and John set standards that made us all proud to be associated with the club."

He often pops up in trivia quizzes with the question: "Who scored a hat-trick against three different Newcastle United goalkeepers?"

It was Alvin who achieved this odd feat in West Ham's freak 8-1 victory over Newcastle in a First Division match in 1986. His first goal was against goalkeeper Martin Thomas, who was then injured. His second and third goals were scored against outfield players Chris Hedworth and Peter Beardsley.

That was the season Hammers finished in their highest ever third place in the top table, and the performances of Martin at the centre of the defence played a vital part in the success.

It would have been easy for Alvin to have demanded a move when West Ham were having their down periods. He was coveted by many managers as a centre-half of true quality, but his soul was with the Hammers and he stayed loyal even when the going got tough.

He had a brief winding-down spell with Leyton Orient before flirting with management at Southend United. But it was his adopted club of West Ham that will always have a special place in his heart … and he will always have a special place in the memories of the fans who enjoyed his determined and dedicated performances.

QUOTE UNQUOTE: Alvin Martin

'Who would have thought that Everton turning me down would do me a favour? I was so fortunate to come under the influence of first Ron Greenwood and then John Lyall. Both shared a vision for the game that demanded it should be played with skill and style, and they made sure all the young players on the books learned that there was a right way and a wrong way to play football. We were fed only good habits. All these years on I remain a West Ham man, and am warmed by the wonderful memories of my days at Upton Park where I was accepted as one of their own. For a Scouser, that was quite something.'

IT is almost impossible to mention the name Alan Devonshire without in the same breath saying Trevor Brooking. Together, they were the brains of the 1980 FA Cup-winning team, merging perfectly with the brawn of the likes of Billy Bonds and David Cross.

Few teams in the land could match the midfield mastery of Devonshire and Brooking, who between them could thread the ball through the tightest of defences.

The mystery is why Brooking went on to collect 47 England caps while the equally gifted Devonshire had to be content with just eight that came in fits and starts.

Ron Greenwood and Bobby Robson were the England managers who selected him, but neither gave him the uninterrupted run he needed to build his confidence at international level. He was unfortunate to be around at the same time as the Tottenham pass master Glenn Hoddle, whose more precise and predictable passing was preferred to his off-the-cuff trickery.

Born: Park Royal
April 13, 1956
Ht 5ft 10.5in Wt 11st

Position:
Central midfield

League games:
West Ham
(1976-90) 358 (29 goals)
Watford (1990-92)
25 (1 goal)
Total:
383 games, 30 goals

8 England caps
(1980-83)

Alan missed the traditional West Ham grounding of an Upton Park apprenticeship. He was discovered at the age of twenty while playing for Southall, and working for his daily bread as a forklift driver in the Hoover factory situated on the A40 on the way into West London. His West Ham-born father, Les, had been a professional with Chester and Crystal Palace, but somehow his son was not picked up on the usual youth football radar.

He had become disillusioned when Malcolm Allison turned him away from Crystal Palace, and he had to be nagged by his Mum and Dad into making the journey across London to start his League career at Upton Park in 1976 for the first of 358 League games in the claret and blue.

From day one there was something enigmatic about Alan's play that was not out of the coaching manual. He was an intuitive touch player, giving and going and expecting an instant return pass.

Most players were not able to match his thought process but, in Brooking, he found a kindred spirit and together they played some absolutely blinding football that was

Alan Devonshire, the Hammer who was full of cunning, stunning running

appreciated and applauded by West Ham fans brought up on a diet of sophisticated football.

His critics claimed that he could not tackle his way out of a paper bag, but winning the ball was not his brief. He left that to physical players like Billy Bonds and, then once in possession, he waved his conductor's baton. As a naturally two-footed player, he could dictate from a central midfield position, or on either flank.

John Lyall said of him: "There are some things that Alan does that cannot be taught. It is purely insticntive, and even he cannot tell you how he did it. It's fascinating to watch him when he's on the ball because you just don't know what to expect next, and when he's not in possession he manages to find space for himself to receive the ball without the opponents knowing where he's gone and why. He and Trevor are like twins with their thinking, and have an understanding that at times is almost eerie. They always seem to know where to be to find each other."

One of Alan's midfield predecessors – Ronnie Boyce – was known as 'Ticker' because he made the Hammers team tick. It was a nickname that would also have suited Alan. He was a creative artist who had a softly-softly approach to his football. Only those with a deeper understanding of the complexities of the 'simple' game fully valued his input.

He was a born maker rather than taker of goals, and scored just 29 in all his League appearances, but his 'assists' ran into the hundreds.

Slowed by niggling injuries and advancing years, he moved to Watford in 1990 for his last bow before starting a long run as an acclaimed non-League manager, first with Maidenhead and then Hampton and Richmond Borough. He took the best things he had learned at the West Ham academy and passed them on to the procession of youngsters, who were starting out in the same sort of non-League environment where he had first blossomed in the 1970s.

If he can unearth another Alan Devonshire he will have found a diamond.

QUOTE UNQUOTE: Alan Devonshire

'I am convinced that the English players around in the 1970s and 1980s had more ability than the youngsters today. It is not good for them that there are so many foreign players filling the first-team places. We played some exceptional football under John Lyall's management. Trevor and I really hit it off. Our understanding came naturally rather than anything that was planned. Trev was a very intelligent man, and we had a sort of telepathy on the pitch. We just seemed to know where the other was at any moment during a game, and knew where to go to get the best out of each other. It was a pleasure to play with him.'

Born: Aveley, Essex
August 28, 1962
Position: Midfield
Ht 5ft 7in, Wt 9st 12lbs

League games:
West Ham (1979-85)
152, 6 goals;
Tottenham (1985-93)
Southampton (1993-95)
Luton (1994 loan) Stoke
(1995 loan) Swindon
(1995-97) Bristol City
(1997) Millwall (1997-98)
Total: 587, 32 goals

3 England Under-23 caps

A HOLLYWOOD scriptwriter would have struggled to come up with a scenario to match the true-life events of Paul Allen in 1979-80. He started the season with his vast footballing family ranged along the touchline watching him in an Under-18 South East Counties match at Chadwell Heath and, he finished it, with the same relatives cheering him on at Wembley in the FA Cup final.

Paul famously became the then youngest ever FA Cup Wembley finalist at 17 years 256 days old when he played for the Hammers against Arsenal on May 10, 1980 (a record since beaten by Millwall's Curtis Weston at 17 years 119 days old).

From the renowned Allen footballing dynasty that also gave us professionals Les and Dennis, Clive, Bradley and Martin, Paul had plenty of advice on his way through his football adventure – wide-ranging experience that equipped him perfectly for the role he now has as an executive for the Professional Footballers' Association.

Paul, with the energy to run all day, was the water carrier for the West Ham team in his first season, winning the ball and then giving it to the senior schemers Brooking and Devonshire to weave their magic.

He had an old head on his young shoulders and could read the game like a seasoned pro, showing that he had grown up in a family steeped in football and been through the star-class education of the West Ham youth academy under the guidance of super-coach Tony Carr (an unsung hero who produced a procession of outstanding youngsters off the West Ham conveyor belt).

John Lyall said of Paul when he first promoted him to the first-team for a League game against Burnley when he was 17 years 32 days old: "I have no worries that Paul can do the job we want. He is very mature for his age, and will not be overawed. He eats, drinks and sleeps football and will be inspired rather than inhibited by the chance to play at the highest level. I would not just throw him in unless I was confident he could handle the occasion. Paul has grown up in a football environment and will, I know, thrive on the occasion."

Paul Allen, an old head on young shoulders

It is part of footballing folklore how Paul collected an FA Cup winners' medal before he was old enough to drive, but the story could have had an even more illustrious page in Wembley history.

He was clean through the Arsenal defence in the closing moments with a goal looking a certainty when Gunners centre-half Willie Young clobbered him with a foul that, today, would have earned him an instant red card. We will give full details in our Cup Final report later in the book, but it speaks volumes for the kind of likable, level-headed character Paul is that he has never once moaned or groaned about the controversial incident.

"Perhaps Willie did me a favour," he says with a smile and a shrug. "Suppose I had missed the chance? That would have been very embarrassing. I was just delighted to have finished on the winning side. It was amazing that just a few months earlier I had been playing in front of a handful of spectators, many of them my relatives, in a South East Counties youth match."

Paul collected a Second Division championship medal with the Hammers in 1980-81 and helped re-establish them as a First Division side before moving on to Tottenham for £400,000 in the summer of 1985. Paul felt in need of a new challenge, and he cemented himself into the Spurs team that reached FA Cup finals in 1987 (runner-up against Coventry) and 1991 (winner against Nottingham Forest). He teamed up with cousin Clive, who scored an astonishing 49 goals in the 1986-87 season, with Paul as one of the supporting players in a five-man midfield.

He later travelled the football roundabout with Southampton, Luton, Stoke, Swindon, Bristol City and Millwall, but will always be associated with West Ham and that 1980 FA Cup appearance. You couldn't make it up.

> ## QUOTE UNQUOTE: Paul Allen
> 'People still constantly mention the 1980 FA Cup final to me, and it is almost as if I only played one game in my career! I remember the kindly John Lyall saying to me that I should just play my normal game, and that I would be comfortable with so many experienced players around me. I had no real fear because at 17 everything just flashes by. Funnily enough I was much more nervous in my last FA Cup final appearance eleven years later. That ended happily too, with a Tottenham victory over Nottingham Forest, despite us losing the great Gazza in the opening minutes.'

Born: Hull
June 21 1949
Ht 5ft 8in. Wt 11st 12lbs

Position:
Striker

League games:
Hull City (1968-74)
Manchester United
(1974-79)
West Ham (1979-82)
34, 6 goals
Total:
302 games, 105 goals

15 England caps, 5 goals

STUART 'PANCHO' PEARSON was damaged goods by the time he arrived at West Ham in the summer of 1979. It was well known in the village world of football that a knee injury suffered in 1978 while playing for Manchester United was so serious that he would never be the same force that had made him a free-scoring favourite at Old Trafford.

Manager John Lyall considered it worth taking a gamble on Pearson's fitness, because he felt his positional play and exquisite passing in crowded penalty areas could bring the best out of striker David Cross. He paid out £220,000 for a player who helped Man United win the FA Cup in 1977 with a goal in the final against Liverpool

Pearson – nicknamed Pancho after former Man United player Mark 'Pancho' Pearson – managed just 34 League games for the Hammers over three years as he battled with his recurring knee problems. Yet, remarkably, he managed to be almost an ever-present in the FA Cup run of 1979-80, and played a major part in Trevor Brooking's famous winning goal against Arsenal. He was twice substituted because of injury.

Pearson had first established himself as a natural goalscorer with his hometown club Hull City. He scored 44 goals in 129 League games for Hull, and got himself in the headlines for the oddest of reasons when sent-off for calling a linesman "a silly bloody onion." Enough to make you weep.

Stocky, and round-shouldered, Pearson was not your run-of-the-mill striker. He was powerful but also cunning, opening up defences with clever decoy runs. Stuart had good close ball control, electric acceleration and could turn half chances into goals because of his quick thinking. Tommy Docherty bought him from Hull for £200,000 to help shoot Man United back to the First Division following their shock relegation in 1974. He popularized a trademark uppercut with his right fist after scoring goals that was copied by parks footballers across the land.

As well as knowing his way to the net, he was expert at bringing team-mates into the action with swift, well-placed passes. Lou Macari, in particular, fed off them at

Stuart Pearson, an ever-present in West Ham's FA Cup-winning team

Manchester United, for whom Pearson plundered 55 goals in 139 League games before the knee injury that threatened a premature end to his career.

He was in the Man United side shocked to a 1-0 defeat by Southampton in the 1976 FA Cup final, and was back the following year to score the first United goal on their way to a 2-1 victory over Liverpool. Tommy Docherty said of him: "I first spotted Stuart when he was a youngster on Hull City's books when I was helping out Terry Neill as assistant manager. I made a mental note to watch his progress, and when I got the Old Trafford job a couple of years later he was one of the first names on the list of players I wanted to sign. He always gives 100 per cent, is an outstanding professional and a good team player who does not care who scores provided the ball goes into the net. He wants the glory for his team, not himself. That's the sort of player a manager dreams about signing."

At his peak, Pearson won fifteen England caps and scored five goals. His international career straddled the reigns of Don Revie and Ron Greenwood. He was played as an out-and-out centre-forward by Revie, while he was best suited to a supporting role alongside a main striker. This was the way he played for West Ham, partnering David Cross and bringing the best out of his robust team-mate with his smart movement on and off the ball. Greenwood was a fan of Pearson's subtle style of play, but his knee injury ended his international ambitions.

Stuart was finally forced out of top-flight football by the knee problem in 1982, but managed to operate for a couple of more seasons in the less demanding football of South Africa and the North American Soccer League.

He returned to England to run a tile-importing business, and coached Stockport County and briefly managed Northwich Victoria before a spell as assistant manager/coach at West Bromwich Albion.

QUOTE UNQUOTE: Stuart Pearson

'I had a frustrating time at West Ham because of my injury problems, but John Lyall was patient with me and gave me every encouragement and motivation. It was great to repay his faith in me by helping the team win the FA Cup in a final most people expected us to lose. John instructed me to play deeper than usual against Arsenal and I think that helped give us an edge because we were outnumbering them in midfield. In the television coverage of the final I am shown as the goalscorer. The camera did not pick up Trevor going down to nod in my mis-hit shot!'

Born: Heywood, Lancs
December 8 1950
Position: Centre-forward
Ht 6ft 1in, Wt 12st 2lbs

League games: Rochdale
(1969-71) Norwich (1971-
73) Coventry (1973-76)
WBA (1976-77)
West Ham (1977-82)
179, 77 goals
Man City (1982-83)
Oldham (1983-84) WBA
(1984-85) Bolton (1985-
86) Bury (1985-86 loan)

Total: 553, 194 goals

DAVID CROSS was refreshingly candid about his job as a striker. "I am there to score goals, so I need to be greedy and single-minded," he said after a four-goal haul against Spurs in a 1981 League Cup tie. "I have to be selfish or I cannot do my job properly."

This statement typified David's honest, no-nonsense approach to the game, and it was this sort of hungry attitude that gave manager John Lyall the confidence to trust him with a special assignment against Arsenal in the 1980 final.

He briefed him to play a lone hunting job up front, with his usual side-kick Stuart Pearson put on a leash in midfield. It was a master tactical stroke that completely flummoxed Arsenal boss Terry Neill and his players.

Bearded Cross ran himself into the ground on a sweltering hot day, enabling West Ham to have an extra man in the middle of the park and so cutting off the supply line to the Arsenal forwards.

An intelligent and articulate man, Lancastrian Cross was a have-boots-will-travel professional hitman who started his football journey at Rochdale before contracts with Norwich City, Coventry City and West Bromwich Albion on his way to West Ham for a fee of £180,000 in 1977. Then, after 77 goals in 179 League games for the Hammers, he was off on his travels again, this time to Manchester City and later to Vancouver Whitecaps, Oldham, back to West Brom, on to Bolton and briefly at Bury before taking his final shots with AEL Limassol in Cyprus.

Everywhere he took his shooting boots, David came up with crucial goals – not always winning the approval of his team-mates because of his self-confessed greed in the penalty area where he would have pushed his granny out of the way to grab a goal.

He had few frills about his game, and just got on with focusing on the only thing that interested him – putting the ball into the back of the net.

It was a method that worked and, by the time he had finished hunting, he had more than 250 goals to his name in all competitions. He was on fire in the season following the FA Cup final triumph, shooting the Hammers back to the First Division with 22

David Cross, who played a lone goal hunter's role in the 1980 FA Cup final

goals and winning the golden boot with 34 goals in total.

Off the pitch, he was nothing like the belligerent and often confrontational player on it, and he had lots of bright thoughts about the tactics and technique of football, which made him ideally suited to the John Lyall school of soccer theory.

He played twice as many games at West Ham than at any of his other clubs, and fitted comfortably into the Hammers football family

David was not only a committed competitor, but also a man of his word. After he had stuffed four goals past goalkeeper Ray Clemence in the League Cup victory at White Hart Lane, he left the ground without the match ball. He explained: "The last time I scored a hat-trick and took the match ball home our goalkeeper Phil Parkes jokingly complained that when he saved three goals nobody gave him the ball. I promised him that next time I scored a hat-trick I would see that he got the ball. So I have just handed it over to him."

When he returned home from playing his final football matches in Cyrpus, David had a period working as a financial adviser for Allied Dunbar in Manchester but the game was too big a pull for him. He joined the coaching staff at Oldham, moving up to assistant manager in 2002, and he then had a brief spell at Blackburn Rovers bringing on the youth players in the style of West Ham's academy run by the renowned Tony Carr.

David, who has two daughters who are international class women's cricketers, later returned to Upton Park in the vital role of chief scout, on the look out for the type of greedy Cross-like forward interested only in putting the ball into the net. That would be like finding gold dust.

QUOTE UNQUOTE: David Cross

'When John Lyall asked me to play the lone striker up front in the 1980 FA Cup final against Arsenal, I took the positive view that it was my chance for Wembley glory. It is no good going into a game of that magnitude with negative thoughts. For a goalscorer, the game is so much about confidence. If you don't have confidence in yourself and a selfish streak you can forget about scoring on a regular basis. The job that John gave me became even more challenging because the final against Arsenal was played in baking-hot conditions. I just kept on running as hard as I could, making sure I was a target for the boys in midfield. Winning the Cup was something I had always dreamt about as a boy, and it was the greatest moment of my career when we won against all the odds. I was completely worn out at the end of the game, but all the effort was worth it.'

S IR TREVOR BROOKING is a living legend at West Ham, the club he served over a stretch of more than 600 matches while always epitomising the spirit of the Hammers – skilful, sporting and sophisticated.

His influence on the game has gone far beyond the boundaries of West Ham, and he was knighted for his administrative services to the Football Association. The 'Centenary Stand' at Upton Park has been named in his honour.

The old cliché about footballers having their brains in their feet was kicked into touch by Trevor, who collected examination honours like trading stamps. While at Ilford County High School he earned 11 O-levels and two A-levels, all this while passing his football exams with honours at the West Ham football academy.

The son of a local police inspector, he transferred his deep intellect to the football field and played with an intelligence and imagination that would have brought him a hatful of honours had he been with a more fashionable team. But Trevor stayed loyal to the Irons and must surely have claret and blue blood coursing through his veins.

His vision and creativity were rewarded with 47 England caps on the international stage, where his double-act with Kevin Keegan was one of the highlights of English football campaigns in the 1970s through to the early '80s. And his partnership for West Ham with Alan Devonshire was just as eye catching and devastating to defences.

Injuries to Brooking and Keegan prevented them from showing their quality in the 1982 World Cup finals when both were in Ron Greenwood's squad but unable to play until coming on as late substitutes in what proved England's final game of the tournament.

For all his talent, Trevor's stunning output for the Hammers did not always breed domestic success and much of his career was spent in relegation struggles or promotion battles to get West Ham back up into the First Division. But he always looked elegant doing it!

Never ever sent-off, Trevor was a true gentleman of the game and an ambassador

Born: Barking, London October 2 1948

Ht 6ft 0.5in, Wt 13st

Position: Midfield

League games: West Ham (1967-84) 528, 88 goals Total West Ham games: 636, 103 goals

47 England caps, 5 goals

It's hands up for Trevor as his goal starts a knees-up for West Ham fans at Wembley

for English football in the Bobby Charlton mould. While playing under his mentor Ron Greenwood and then his friend John Lyall he always exemplified the West Ham obligation – compulsion even – to play the game in the right spirit.

Trevor was brighter than the average off as well as on the field, and was always entrepreneurial. Virtually throughout his career he ran a book-binding and print finishing company with an old Ilford County High schoolfriend, Colin McGowan. It is called Colbrook Plastics Limited, is based in Essex and Sir Trevor continues to monitor the running of the the 40-year-old company.

But it was football that took his main focus, and he gave West Ham 100 per cent in effort and concentration after a spell on the transfer list following frustration early in his career. This was when West Ham were in a transitional period after their cup successes of the mid-1960s, and Trevor was never sure of his place in the team.

The fact that he scored West Ham's winning goal in the 1980 final causes amazement and amusement in equal measure, even thirty years on. Trevor was the master of the driving mazy runs from deep positions, bewildering defenders with his subtle changes of feet and pace. The ball used to seem tied to his boots, and he could land his passes on a sixpence. But heading the ball? That was one of the few arts that eluded him. He thought his head was for putting his England caps on.

Brian Clough famously said of him before the 1980 final: "Trevor Brooking floats like a butterfly and stings like one …"

The fact that he scored the winning goal – and with his head – was the most satisfying moment of his career, and silenced Cloughie and all those critics who claimed that he decorated rather than decided matches.

Trevor has since, of course, become a household name as a broadcaster, administrator and leading spokesperson on all things to do with English football at the top level. He has had two brief, successful spells as emergency manager at Upton Park where he is hugely respected and revered.

He continues to be a great advertisement for what can be achieved at the West Ham academy. Go to the top of the class (again), Sir Trevor.

> **QUOTE UNQUOTE: Sir Trevor Brooking**
> 'No matter what, West Ham will always be my club. It is in my bones, in my blood. I deal these days with football at all levels, but wherever I go people want to talk to me about West Ham, and in particular that headed goal against Arsenal at Wembley. I am very happy to be so closely associated with a club where I had the best years of my life.'

Born: Lower Clapton, London
September 28 1956

Ht 5ft 7in, Wt 11st 12lbs
Position: Midfield

League games:
West Ham (1975-87)
291, 32 goals
Notts County (1987-89)
Leyton Orient (1989-91)

Total: 417, 50 goals

GEOFF who? Don't tell him your name, Pike! Ask 100 West Ham fans to name the 1980 FA Cup line-up, and Geoff's will be the name many will struggle to come up with. This is true but also unfair, because his input to the FA Cup success was as important as anybody else's in what was very much a team triumph.

Would Geoff have made the side if Jimmy Neighbour and/or Pat Holland had not been injured? That is one of the great imponderables, but the reality is that Geoff played in every minute of seven of the eight FA Cup ties including the final, and also came on to give substitute input to the other game.

Discovered playing with Gidea Park Rangers, Geoff was on West Ham's books from the age of ten, when John Lyall was his coach. He signed for the Irons straight from school and was in the team that reached the 1975 FA Youth Cup final. John Lyall wanted him to broaden his game and sent him on loan to Connecticut Bicentennials in the North American Soccer League to get extra experience after he had made his League debut against Birmingham City in March 1976.

While in the States he played against the giants of the game like Pele, Eusebio and Franz Beckenbauer and learned things he could never have picked up in the English league.

By the time he returned to Upton Park, he was a vastly improved player and over the next twelve years gave the Hammers magnificent service while playing more than 300 League and Cup games.

Geoff was a players' player, working like a beaver in midfield without taking the plaudits, but appreciated by his team-mates who knew he was the hidden ace in the pack. His strengths were his stamina, his speed in short bursts, his support play of whichever of his colleagues was in possession and a fierce competitive spirit that meant he never threw in the towel no matter how tough and demanding the action became.

He was right at the heart of the Hammers as they captured the FA Cup in 1980, the Second Division championship in 1980-81 and finished League Cup runners-up in the same season. His all-round skills were on show when he played the role of emergency

Geoff Pike, a players' player who was the hidden ace in the West Ham pack

centre-forward in the third round FA Cup replay againt West Brom, and scored a crucial goal. 'Mr Reliable,' he was mainly a ball winner and a disciplined man marker, but scampered through to steal 32 goals in his 291 League appearances over a span of a dozen years. He played in three Wembley finals in the space of just ten months (four times, if you include the Charity Shield). As well as the FA Cup final, he appeared in the League Cup final against Liverpool in 1981 and then the replay after a 1-1 draw. It was the general concensus that he had been one of West Ham's most productive players across the two games against the mighty Merseysiders

To this day, Geoff remembers Alan Kennedy's controversial opening goal for Liverpool. "Sammy Lee was way off-side," Greg recalls. "Referee Clive Thomas waved aside our protests. John Lyall was the calmest of men but even he blew his top over that one. It was justice when Ray Stewart scored his superbly taken last minute equaliser from the penalty spot."

While it was ball masters like Brooking and Devonshire who took the eye, it was the selfless running, fetching and carrying of a dedicated professional like Geoff that enabled them to find the time and space in which to do the defence-demolition work. He was runner-up to Phil Parkes in the 1981 Hammer of the Year vote.

Geoff left his second home of Upton Park in 1987 to play for Notts County and scored 17 goals in 82 League games before returning to London for two wind-down seasons with Leyton Orient. He later passed on all he had learned as a regional coach for the PFA before taking a managerial responsibility for grassroots development of the game with the Football Association, working closely with his old team-mate Sir Trevor Brooking. Nobody needs to say Geoff Who? Pike's the name, and quality coaching is his game. His name shines brightly in the West Ham history book, and in the best traditions of the Hammers academy he continues to give something back to the game that he served so well as a player.

QUOTE UNQUOTE: Geoff Pike

'The West Ham years were as good as it gets, particularly when we won the FA Cup and promotion the following season. Our manager John Lyall had to take much of the credit. He got the balance of the team just right. As a coach, a person, a manager, as well as a man, he was a massive influence on me and most of the young players at the club. When I joined the club as a ten-year-old in the World Cup year of 1966 he was the youth team coach and he was the best possible successor to Ron Greenwood as manager. I have taken much of what he taught me into my coaching career.'

JOHN LYALL selected 15 players on the way to Wembley for the 1980 FA Cup final against Arsenal. Defender **Paul Brush** was the unluckiest to lose out after playing in six full ties and substituting in another. He finished up on the bench back in the days when only one substitute was allowed. Paul wore the number 12 shirt and did not get a kick. John Lyall went out of his way to acknowledge his contribution to the Cup success.

Born within the crowd roar of Upton Park in Plaistow on February 22 1958, Paul came through the West Ham youth academy and was a fringe member of the first team squad at the age of nineteen in 1977. He lost out when Ray Stewart arrived, but then filled his favourite No 3 shirt when Frank Lampard moved across to right-back, allowing Stewart to play an anchorman role in midfield.

Paul played 151 League games for the Hammers before switching in 1985 to Crystal Palace and then Southend, followed by non-League action with Enfield and Heybridge Swifts. He later had two years as Orient manager, and was assistant manager to Steve Tilson at Southend from 2004 until the spring of 2010.

Patsy Holland was an immensely popular and competitive midfielder-come-winger for West Ham from 1969 to 1981 until injury forced a premature retirement just as the Irons were coming to their peak under John Lyall's management.

Born in Poplar on September 13 1950, Patsy played in the winning 1975 FA Cup team against Fulham and scored 23 goals in a total 245 League games for the Hammers. In the crucial 1979-80 season he made 26 League appearances and played in just the first semi-final against Everton before knee problems terminated his career.

He had a brief flirtation with management at Leyton Orient, and he coached at Queens Park Rangers, Tottenham and Millwall before becoming a scout for the Lions and then the MK Dons.

When it was clear that Pat Holland was struggling for fitness, John Lyall paid £150,000 to bring in **Jimmy Neighbour** from Norwich City. He had made a name for himself as a winger with Tottenham, helping them win the League Cup in 1971. Born in Chingford on November 15 1950, he was a traditional old school winger until developing into a midfield flank player who had pace and excellent dribbling skills.

He played 97 games in total for the Hammers, including four appearances on the FA Cup trail. One of the six goals he scored for the Irons was a dramatic far-post

An impressionist's view of Tottenham's Steve Archibald under pressure from Paul Brush

winner against Coventry City that clinched West Ham's place in the 1981 League Cup final. He was similar to Patsy Holland in both his playing style and likable personality, and won instant affection from the claret and blue fans.

In 1983 he had a six match spell on loan at Bournemouth, then played two games for Isthmian League side Cheshunt before coaching at Enfield. He returned to West Ham in the role of Youth Development Officer, and took a similar assignment at Tottenham after managerial jobs at Doncaster Rovers and St Albans City.

He was monitoring games for the Premier League in 2009 and still closely involved with the game that he loved when, aged 58, he died suddenly following a heart attack.

Jimmy was much-mourned throughout football.

The only other player who made it into the FA Cup frame for the Hammers in the 1979-80 season was **Dale Banton**, a forward who was the non-playing substitute against West Bromwich Albion in the third round. Born in Kensington on May 15 1961, he came through the Hammers youth academy and played just five League games before moving in 1982 to Aldershot for whom he scored 47 goals in 106 League appearances.

West Ham's Road to Wembley started at The Hawthorns on January 5 1980 ...

West Bromwich Albion 1, West Ham United 1

WEST HAM were just twenty-six seconds away from dispatching First Division opponents West Bromwich Albion at the start of their FA Cup adventure when Cyrille Regis scored a goal of such controversy that it could be measured on the Richter scale.

To a man, the Hammers defenders protested that Regis had controlled the ball with his hand before he drove an unstoppable shot past Phil Parkes for a dramatic last-kick equaliser that clearly should have been disallowed.

The home fans at The Hawthorns and the Albion players celebrated like prisoners on death row getting a last minute reprieve, while the travelling West Ham army roared their rage as they watched their heroes sinking to their haunches in despair. They'd had victory snatched from them by a goal as dodgy as a nine-bob note.

Even West Brom manager Ron Atkinson conceded the goal should not have counted. "It certainly looked like handball to me," he admitted, "but I am mightily relieved that we are still in the competition. Upton Park is never an easy place to visit and we know we are going to have to be at the top of our game to win the replay."

Only those watching the match through claret-and-blue glasses could deny that West Brom deserved to survive. They were the superior side for most of the game and West Ham's defence was continually exposed to the perils of panic.

One man stood between Albion and a decisive victory. Take a bow Phil Parkes, who played one of the great games of his life.

Without exaggeration, he prevented at least five certain goals with saves that were in the magnificent category. "That's as good a goalkeeping display as I've seen for years," said Atkinson. "We would have had the game wrapped up ages before our equaliser but for the brilliance of Parkes."

John Lyall agreed. "Phil gave a world class performance," he said. "He lifted the spirits of our lads and they worked twice as hard to try to win the game to reward Phil for his fantastic work. I cannot remember seeing a better display by any goalkeeper."

The Hammers defenders were given a chasing by the quick and tricky Peter Barnes, continually switching wings and teasing and tormenting first Ray Stewart at right-back and then Frank Lampard on the other flank.

In the middle, Alvin Martin had his hands full with the powerful runs of Regis, who peppered the West Ham goal with blistering shots that were continually caught, punched or tipped wide by the acrobatic Parkes.

Then Parkes broke the heart of Baggies free-kick specialist Gary Owen, who was

Cyrille Regis, the West Brom powerhouse, gave a more than handy performance against West Ham

ready to celebrate a goal after harrassed Billy Bonds had conceded a free-kick when he brought down dangerman Regis just outside the box. Owen hit a perfect shot that was arrowing towards the far corner when Parkes took off like Superman and pushed the ball around the post. It was a staggering save that earned the grudging applause even of the Albion fans.

Just as the West Brom players were accepting that they were going to have to go in at the end of a one-sided first-half with West Ham on equal terms, they were rocked by a Hammers goal out of nowhere.

Trevor Brooking and Alan Devonshire – the best double-act in the Second Division – suddenly made their entrance on to the stage after being largely redundant. They exchanged the sort of smart passes familiar to the West Ham faithful before Brooking stroked the ball through to Stuart Pearson, who instantly turned it past the wrong-footed goalkeeper Tony Godden from close range. Astonishingly, West Ham were in front from Pearson's first positive touch of the ball.

The second-half was as one-sided as the first, but now West Ham had a lead to protect and there was a new bounce in their step and added bite to their challenges against one of the First Division's most potent attacking forces.

Albion threw everything but the kitchen sink at the team that was seventh in the Second Division to their eighteenth place in the First. Hammers, missing injured striker David Cross, packed their midfield, leaving Pearson to patrol alone in the Albion territory. Left-back Derek Statham hammered in a long-range shot that had 'goal' written all over it until that man Parkes stretched across goal to divert it, and then Peter Barnes looked on disbelievingly as the giant goalkeeper dived full length to pluck his powerful drive out of the air. West Ham were reduced to the foreign-to-them tactics of kicking the ball anywhere as the pressure increased in the closing stages.

Just as they thought they had survived all that Albion could throw at them, Regis clearly brought the ball under control with his hand as he made yet another electric burst through the middle of the Hammers defence. The referee had been looking at his watch as the seconds ticked down. Perhaps that is why he did not see the handball. But what were his linesmen doing? Everybody else in the ground seemed to have seen it and there were yells of "handball" from the players and the travelling West Ham fans. Almost as if in slow motion, Regis took careful aim and rifled in a fierce right-foot shot that even the Great Wall that was Parkes could not stop.

There was time left only for West Ham to restart the match as the final whistle blew to signal that they would have to do it all over again at Upton Park the following Tuesday. Virtually every player on the pitch shook Phil Parkes by the hand as the modest giant walked off at the end. Tony Godden, the Albion goalkeeper who had been a spectator for most of the game, applauded his rival. Sportsmanship was alive and well at The Hawthorns.

THE MATCH FACTS

West Bromwich Albion 1, West Ham United 1

Half-time 0-1

Scorers: Stuart Pearson (West Ham)

Cyrille Regis (West Bromwich)

Attendance: 20,572

WEST BROMWICH ALBION	WEST HAM UNITED
1 Tony Godden	1 Phil Parkes
2 Brendon Batson	2 Ray Stewart
3 Derek Statham	3 Frank Lampard
4 John Trewick	4 Billy Bonds
5 John Wile	5 Alvin Martin
6 Alistair Robertson	6 Alan Devonshire
7 John Deehan	7 Paul Allen
8 Alistair Brown	8 Stuart Pearson
9 Cyrille Regis	9 Geoff Pike
10 Gary Owen	10 Trevor Brooking
11 Peter Barnes	11 Jimmy Neighbour
12 Tony Brown	12 Dale Banton

Man of the match: Phil Parkes

PHIL PARKES: "I had one of those days when I managed to get in the way of everything ... except that last-minute shot from Cyrille. I was too busy watching for his shot to worry about whether he had handled the ball, but all the rest of the lads said he definietly did. It was a choker for their goal to come so late in the game after we had kept them out for so long. Ron Atkinson congratulated me on my performance, hich was nice of him. Now we have to get ourself up for the replay. West Brom have a better attack than any side we play in the Second Division, so we have it all to do at Upton Park."

CYRILLE REGIS: "The ball may have brushed my hand, but it was not deliberate and I guess that's the way the ref saw it. I have seen few better goalkeeping displays than that by Phil Parkes today. He was outstanding. Any other day I would have had at least a hat-trick. I almost felt like applauding some of his saves but that might have encouraged him to do it again. We are very confident we can win at their place, because we proved today that we are the better team by at least three goals. We hav a team capable of winning the Cup, but first we've got to get past West Ham."

BILLY BONDS: "Okay, West Brom did not deserve to lose but that doesn't mean we have to lie down and accept a goal that should have been ruled out. Cyrille handled the ball. No question. `On today's showing, Phil is not just the best goalkeeper in the country but in the world. The big feller has kept us in the Cup. Now we have to make all his effort worthwhile by going all out to win the replay at Upton Park, where our fans are going to play a huge part."

JOHN LYALL: "I do not have the words to describe that performance by Phil. It was just phenomenal. At times he was playing West Brom almost on his own, and the West Brom forwards just could not believe that he ball was not flying into the net. We must tighten up considerably if we are to win the replay and not allow Albion so much possession..Our main target this season is promotion back to the First Division, so a replay is not what we wanted. To say the least, it is going to be interesting at Upton Park."

The day Jimmy Neighbour was welcomed to West Ham by John Lyall, pencilled for posterity

West Ham United 2, West Bromwich Albion 1

GEOFF PIKE, usually the butler carrying and delivering the ball for others, was lord of the manor in a riveting third round replay that had Upton Park in knees-up mood. Wearing the number nine shirt in place of injured David Cross but marauding from midfield, it was Pike who inspired West Ham to an improbable victory over a West Brom team still kicking themselves for not having sewn up the game in the ridiculously one-sided first match.

The pre-match signs were not good. As well as David Cross, West Ham were having to go into action without the barnstorming Billy Bonds.

"I am choked to have to miss the game," the Hammers skipper said. "I told Parksie on Saturday that I felt our name was on the Cup after he had kept us alive, now I'm having to watch the replay. It's going to be murder sitting on the sidelines."

John Lyall assigned Paul Brush to take on the dismantling Bonzo role alongside Alvin Martin, and the always-willing Geoff Pike was given the dual task of helping to shore up the midfield and getting forward to support Stuart Pearson.

Phil Parkes was again in commanding form, but not nearly as busy as he had been at The Hawthorns. This was because the Hammers defenders followed the Lyall instructions to be tighter and more tigerish with their marking and more deliberate with their challenges. Cyrille Regis, who had threatened to run riot against them on the Saturday, found his space restricted by the combined efforts of Alvin Martin and Paul Brush, who performed valiantly in place of the sidelined Bonds.

Peter Barnes had found acres of freedom at The Hawthorns, but was kept under lock and key by the more disciplined defensive play of Ray Stewart and Frank Lampard. Whichever wing he tried, Barnes had claret and blue shadows forcing him into cul de sacs.

There was a hidden extra man – the West Ham crowd. They continually lifted the players to additional effort with their fanatical, deafening support as ten thousand more spectators crammed into Upton Park than had attended the first game at West Brom. If you had watched the game not knowing which side was which, you would have been convinced that the Hammers were the First Division team. They played some exquisite football, making the Albion defend in numbers in a match that was a complete contrast to the Saturday encounter.

Trevor Brooking and Alan Devonshire were bossing the game from midfield, passing the ball with accuracy and penetration. Jimmy Neighbour was continually making tricky and threatening runs down the left wing, and Stuart Pearson was proving a powerful presence in the Albion penalty area.

You could almost see the question written on the faces of the West Brom players: "Is this the same team that we outplayed on Saturday …?"

West Ham at Upton Park are always a different proposition than the travelling Hammers. They seem to grow in stature and strength the moment they feel the Boleyn turf under their boots and the roar of the home fans in their ears.

The Irons gave an early indication of their intentions when Geoff Pike headed the ball into the net in the sixth minute, but referee John Hunting ruled it out because Alvin Martin had clearly obstructed goalkeeper Tony Godden. A pity the referee had not been as sharp-eyed and on the ball when Regis committed his handling offence in the first game!

Godden took over the Parkes role of saviour, diving courageously at the feet of Stuart Pearson as the Hammers striker shaped to shoot a certain goal, and moments later he arched backwards to tip over another Pike header.

Standing only 5ft 7in tall, 22-year-old Pike was giving a giant-hearted performance against the towering Albion defenders. He was playing with dynamic energy as if he had an extra lung.

It was the Baggies who were clinging on for dear life at the end of a goalless first-half that was definitely won on points by the inspired Hammers, and just seven minutes after the interval they took the lead they deserved.

The immaculate Brooking came smoothly forward from the packed midfield and swept a pin-pointed pass into the path of the industrious Pike, who gleefully guided the ball wide of the oncoming Godden. It suddenly sounded as if there were 300,000 rather than 30,000 spectators in the ground, and the choruses of Bubbles could have been heard on Mars.

Startled West Brom sent on their veteran marksman Tony Brown in place of Gary Owen in a bid to snatch an equaliser, but they left themselves open to a counter attack as they pushed forward against a Second Division West Ham side playing First Division-quality football.

West Brom's defence was open as a barn door as Alan Devonshire made ground down the left flank in the 84th minute before pulling the ball back for his regular accomplice Trevor Brooking to drill in a shot that Godden could only wave to on its way into the net.

The cheers of the West Ham fans were still filling the night air when West Brom got brief hope of forcing extra-time. Peter Barnes at last delivered a telling cross from the left and Tony Brown rose to beat Parkes with a well-directed header.

But it was too little too late, and Hammers held out for a famous victory that sent a surge of optimism shooting through the club. Could it really be, as Billy Bonds had forecast on the Saturday, that West Ham's name was on the Cup?

THE MATCH FACTS

West Ham United 2, West Bromwich Albion 1
Half-time 0-0
Scorers: Geoff Pike, Trevor Brooking (West Ham)
Tony Brown (West Bromwich Albion)
Attendance: 30,689
Teams:

WEST HAM UNITED	WEST BROMWICH ALBION
1 Phil Parkes	1 Tony Godden
2 Ray Stewart	2 Brendon Batson
3 Frank Lampard	3 Derek Statham
4 Paul Brush	4 John Trewick
5 Alvin Martin	5 John Wile
6 Alan Devonshire	6 Alistair Robertson
7 Paul Allen	7 John Deehan
8 Stuart Pearson	8 Alistair Brown
9 Geoff Pike	9 Cyrille Regis
10 Trevor Brooking	10 Gary Owen
11 Jimmy Neighbour	11 Peter Barnes
	12 Tony Brown

Man of the match: Geoff Pike

Ron Atkinson, West Brom manager who agreed West Ham deserved their third round replay victory

JOHN LYALL: "We were rewarded for doing the basic things correctly. Some of our possession football in midfield was of the highest quality, and caused West Brom a lot of frustration. You can only play if you have the ball and we continually denied them it, unlike on Saturday when we were loose with our marking. I don't like picking out individuals because this was a victory for teamwork, but I have to praise Geoff Pike who ran his legs off and got the goal he deserved for all his effort. Our main concentration has still got to be on the League, but an FA Cup run would be a welcome bonus."

RON ATKINSON: "Hats off to West Ham, they thoroughly earned their victory. We threw it away at home, when we could and should have won by three or four goals. When they write the history of this FA Cup year they must remember to give Phil Parkes the credit for keeping West Ham alive on Saturday. Our players stopped using their heads tonight, and allowed West Ham to crowd them out. It will be interesting to see how far they can go in the Cup this year. It could be a long way."

GEOFF PIKE: "I wore the number nine shirt but could hardly be called a centre-forward. It was my intention to make myself a nuisance in the penalty area in an effort to make room for Stuart to put the ball away. My goal was laid on a plate for me by Trevor's wonderfully placed pass, and once we got into the lead you could almost see the confidence draining out of the West Brom players. They knew their best victory chance had disappeared at The Hawthorns. There is a great spirit in our dressing-room and we all sense we just might be able to have a Cup run."

TREVOR BROOKING:"When the second goal went in I knew we had got our ticket into the next round. While I put it into the net, Alan deserves a lot of the credit for the way he calmly picked me out with a perfect ball. We kept our composure when West Brom hit back with their goal, but the last few minutes seemed to take forever. It was a relief to get it over in 90 minutes. Extra-time would have been exhausting because we had given everything to get the win we deserved. Yesterday's fourth round draw has given us the short journey to Leyton Orient, which is a tricky match. But there is a confidence throughout the team that we can make it into the fifth round, and then anything is possible."

Orient 2, West Ham United 3

AS the Duke of Wellington said after the Battle of Waterloo: "It was a damn close run thing …" Brave and unbowed Orient gave their more illustrious neighbours one hell of a fright and a fight before finally conceding defeat in a five-goal thriller at Brisbane Road.

Orient had ambitions way above their Third Division status, and there was a familiar look to their side. Ex-Hammers Tommy Taylor and Billy Jennings formed the spine of the team at centre-half and centre-forward, and only injury prevented goalkeeper Mervyn Day from being between the sticks against his old club. All three had played for West Ham in the 1975 FA Cup final triumph over Fulham. Jimmy Bloomfield, once a West Ham schemer, was the Orient manager, who had steered the Os to the FA Cup semi-final in 1978.

Former Tottenham maestro Ralph Coates was their midfield marshal, and in flying Nigerian John Chiedozie they had one of the most dangerous wingers in the League.

Hammers were in confident mood after a 2-0 win against Preston the previous week had lifted them to sixth place in the table, but John Lyall warned gravely about the dangers of complacency.

"We were the giant killers against West Brom," he said. "Now it's our heads that are on the block if we don't give the game our full attention."

The Hammers were still without David Cross, and there was a huge blow for them when a muscle strain kept schemer-in-chief Trevor Brooking on the sidelines. Lyall shuffled the pack to let utility defender Paul Brush in at right-back and switched Ray Stewart to a holding position in midfield.

Billy Bonds led the team out looking like John Cleese in the 'Don't mention the war' episode of Fawlty Towers. His head was swathed in a huge bandage following a succession of injuries that had the medics suggesting that he should sit this one out, but action man Bonzo would not hear of it. He played with all his usual fire and commitment, and got himself booked for one wild challenge as the jet-heeled Chiedozie threatened to make fools of the West Ham defenders with his unpredictable but stunning running.

It was Orient who took the lead in the eleventh minute, shortly after debutant goalkeeper Sean Rafter had saved brilliantly from an Alan Devonshire snap shot. Billy Bonds handled a cross from ex-Spur Ian Moores, and it was Orient skipper Tommy Taylor who stepped up to score from the spot against his former team.

Tommy Taylor in his West Ham days, a key member of the 1975 FA Cup-winning team

There was a touch of luck to West Ham's equaliser in the twenty-seventh minute. Jimmy Neighbour centred and Geoff Pike's header glanced off Orient defender Nigel Gray and into the net for an own goal.

Seven minutes later it was Ray Stewart's turn to take a penalty after Moores had handled during a spell of heavy West Ham pressure. Ray produced one of his trademark blasts from the spot that would have taken goalkeeper Rafter's head off if he'd got in the way.

There was no question that West Ham were the superior side in the first-half, but the Os came out for the second-half inspired by a team talk from Jimmy Bloomfield who later revealed that he had told them: "If each of you ups your game by ten per cent we can swing the game our way. They may have the edge in skill, but extra effort will cancel that out. We can win this, you've got to believe it."

The Bloomfield forecast began to gather strength when Orient pulled level with the goal of the game. Moores collected a pass from Taylor, ghosted past two West Ham challenges out on the left and then delivered the ball to Chiedozie, who brilliantly chipped the ball home from deep inside the box. It was a goal of pure class.

There was a scare for the Hammers in the seventy-third minute when Billy Jennings had the ball in the net, but the flag was up for off-side. What a sickener that would have been for West Ham, who had sold Billy to the Os for their club record fee of £100,000 just the previous summer.

West Ham were missing the steadying influence of Trevor Brooking, and Alan Devonshire looked a far less effective player without his scheming partner.

A hectic, helter-skelter match was finally decided nine minutes from the end when Stewart advanced from a deep position to collect an Orient clearance. The Os defenders waited for him to pass, but Ray had other ideas and produced a sudden shot that caught Rafter by surprise and flew into the net to make it 3-2. A veteran reporter in the press box said what Jimmy Bloomfield must have been thinking: "Mervyn Day would have eaten that for breakfast."

Gallant Orient refused to throw in the towel and produced a tide of attacks that challenged the composure of the Hammers defence. Phil Parkes, as ever, was the epitome of calm while all about him were losing their heads, and he broke Orient hearts with two difficult saves that he made look easy.

Jimmy Neighbour was threatening to create a victory-clinching fourth goal for the Hammers in a swift counter-attack when he was caught in a half-Nelson by Bill Roffey, a Big Daddy impersonation that earned the Orient defender a booking.

As the final whistle blew, the cheers from the huge army of West Ham supporters who had made the short journey to Leyton were tinged with relief, and they saved a lot of their applause for a brave Orient display that, in truth, deserved the bonus of a replay.

THE AFTER-MATCH QUOTES

JIMMY BLOOMFIELD: "I am so proud of my players. They have given the game everything, and if the Gods had been smiling on us we would have been rewarded with at least a replay. There must have been half a dozen occasions when John Chiedozie cut their defence wide open, and we just lacked that finishing touch that would have put us totally in command. We were fortunate not to be more goals down at half-time, but I thought we were the better team through much of the second-half and it was West Ham who were clinging on at the end. We wish West Ham a long run in the Cup. John Lyall is one of the gentleman of the game and deserves any success that comes his way."

JOHN LYALL: "As I anticipated, Orient gave us a heck of a fight. This was their Cup final and they had us rocking for long periods. It was good to see Tommy Taylor, who still has many friends at West Ham. He was a great pro for us, and is now doing a fine job for the Os. Much as I like him, though, I didn't want to see him leading Orient to victory! You can only go so far with friendship. I don't know how far we're going to go in the Cup, but we won't get many tougher matches than this one. Orient played out of their skins, and I could not have complained had it gone to another replay."

TOMMY TAYLOR: "We gave it our best shot and there were times when we had West Ham really worried. As I took my penalty I tried not to think that it was Phil Parkes on the goal-line, but then as I looked up he seemed as wide as Mount Everest! I was so relieved to get the ball past him. I was hoping we could at least squeeze a replay out of this. It would have been wonderful for me to lead a team out at Upton Park. The Os and the Hammers will always be a big part of me."

RAY STEWART: "I didn't stop to think about my shot that gave us the victory. It was an instinctive thing and I was delighted when the ball hit the back of the net. Orient gave us a scare and on their second-half performance can consider themselves unlucky not to have got a replay. As for the penalty, that's the sort of thing I do dozens of times in training. I concentrate on a combination of power and accuracy, and it's always satisfying when it comes off."

Ray Stewart, the penalty king who was as tough as Aberdeen granite

THE MATCH FACTS

Orient 2, West Ham United 3
Half-time 1-2
Scorers: Tommy Taylor (pen), John Chiedozie (Orient)
Nigel Gray (own goal), Ray Stewart 2, 1 pen (West Ham)
Attendance: 21,521
Teams:

ORIENT	WEST HAM UNITED
1 Sean Rafter	1 Phil Parkes
2 Bobby Fisher	2 Paul Brush
3 Bill Roffey	3 Frank Lampard
4 Tommy Taylor	4 Billy Bonds
5 Nigel Gray	5 Alvin Martin
6 Ian Moores	6 Alan Devonshire
7 John Chiedozie	7 Paul Allen
8 Henry Hughton	8 Stuart Pearson
9 Billy Jennings	9 Geoff Pike
10 John Margerrison	10 Ray Stewart
11 Ralph Coates	11 Jimmy Neighbour

Man of the match: Ray Stewart

West Ham United 2, Swansea City 0

DAVID CROSS was at last fit to make his entry on to the FA Cup stage – and he did it in swashbuckling style, creating one goal and then magnificently scoring a second. All this came in sixty seconds of impulsive inspiration that sank Swansea, just as they were thinking of a money-spinning replay at Vetch Field.

As hard as John Lyall tried to keep the focus on the all-important efforts to get into the Second Division promotion places, he could not stop the waves of Cup fever that were engulfing the Hammers fans who could smell a repeat of their 1975 FA Cup glory.

For the first time since the Cup run began he could put the name of David Cross down as his main striker. That was the good news. The bad news that once again skipper Billy Bonds was sidelined.

Lyall moved Ray Stewart into Bonzo's place, switched Frank Lampard to right-back, Paul Brush into the No 3 shirt and put the prodigy Paul Allen on the substitute's bench. Geoff Pike wore No 11, but with his usual brief of spending most of his time as a water carrier in midfield.

The evidence that West Ham were missing the authority and aggression of Bonzo is that Swansea had long periods when they were in command.

The Swans were six places below West Ham in the Second Division table, and had been beaten 2-0 at Upton Park three months before this tense and dramatic fifth round Cup tie, a game crucial to the financial well-being of both clubs.

Player-manager John Toshack, once the idol of Anfield, knew the odds were stacked against his side, and he came up with a plan to stifle the Hammers attack based on the experience of the League defeat in November.

He played Welsh international Leighton Phillips as a sweeper behind towering central defenders Jeremy Charles and Nigel Stevenson, and he instructed his midfielders to sit tight on main West Ham creators Trevor Brooking and Alan Devonshire. It meant the game became a war of attrition rather than the sort of free-flowing football to which the West Ham faithful were accustomed.

A feature of the game was the struggle for supremacy in midfield, with Alan Devonshire and Trevor Brooking pitting their wits against cagey former Anfield hero Ian Callaghan, supported by another Welsh international in Robbie James.

Once a quick, ball-playing winger who was in England's 1966 World Cup squad, Cally had switched to midfield conductor and it was fascinating to watch him trying to outmanoeuvre the West Ham pass masters. He may have been on old legs, but his mind was still sharp and he provided a silver service of passes to his enthusiastic Swansea team-mates.

With Callaghan in the ascendancy, West Ham's back four took a battering as Swansea searched for a goal, and it was only the safe hands of Phil Parkes that saved them from being at least one down in a grim, goalless first-half. One of his saves from a piledriver shot by James had the Swansea players and fans shaking their heads in disbelief. It was not only West Brom hearts broken by the big man.

West Ham's best goal scoring chances of the first forty-five minutes fell first to Frank Lampard and then David Cross. Following a long overlapping run, Frank was foiled by Swans goalkeeper Glan Letheran, who threw himself at his feet to smother the ball. Then he dived to his near post to grasp an on-target header from Cross, who was having a frustrating time against the heavily packed Swansea defence.

Paul Allen was summoned into the action immediately after the interval when Stuart Pearson was forced to go off with a neck injury, which meant another reshuffling for the Hammers as they struggled to find their usual rhythm and penetration.

Although missing his partner Billy Bonds, Alvin Martin was exceptional at the heart of the defence as Swansea picked up the pace in the second-half. He continually got the better of Toshack both on the ground and in the air, and he earned the applause of his team-mates as his sliding tackle robbed David Giles of what looked to be a clear scoring chance.

Swansea's suffocating defensive tactics worked for 85 minutes, but just as they were thinking of a replay on their home territory the previously subdued Cross produced his two moments of magic.

First of all he unleashed a volley of blistering power that goalkeeper Letheran could only parry, and the alert Paul Allen pounced to put the loose ball into the net.

Then, just a minute later, Cross conjured a goal that had the two elements of bravery and brilliance.

Jimmy Neighbour, who had been hitting the Welsh wall for most of the game, escaped his marker, sprinted into space and sent the ball into the heavily populated penalty area. Cross hurled himself full length to meet the centre with a bullet header and he was still horizontal to the ground as the ball bulged the net. It was concussive and conclusive for the visitors from Wales.

Suddenly Swansea, from thinking of a replay in the Valleys, were now in a valley of despair and wondering how they were 2-0 down.

The dual responsibility of playing and managing was clearly taking its toll on Toshack, who held his head in despair as Cross headed in the match-settling second goal. As he trudged off at the end he could be seen talking animatedly to his defenders … and it was not praise that he was handing out. Football's a cruel old game.

John Toshack, devastated by the 2-0 Swansea City defeat at Upton Park

THE AFTER-MATCH QUOTES

DAVID CROSS: "I'm so pleased that I have at last been able to give something to the team in this Cup run. It's been frustrating to sit on the sidelines watching the lads playing their hearts out, knowing there was nothing I could do to help. It was a great save by the goalkeeper from my shot, and Paul showed excellent reflexes to put the ball away. For the header, I could see what Jimmy was thinking and positioned myself to make sure I could get on the end of it. It was an instinctive thing to throw myself at the ball and I connected perfectly. There's a real buzz in the dressing-room and the fact that we're in the quarter-finals means dreaming of Wembley is not too far-fetched."

JOHN TOSHACK: "There's not a lot I want to say. I am devastated. My plans worked perfectly until we suddenly played like novices and lost our concentration. It was sickening. Dreadful. A replay was there, we had done all the hard work. West Ham are a superb attacking side, yet we had hardly given them a glimpse of our goal. Then we allowed Cross the freedom of the penalty area, not once but twice. To say I am furious is an understatement."

JOHN LYALL: "I will be the first to admit we did not play well, and Swansea deserved at least a replay. But that's football for you. It is a game of 90 minutes and we kept plugging away and made things happen in the end. I was delighted for David, who has been unlucky with injuries. His second goal was a blinder. You don't see too many diving headers like that in the modern game. Alvin Martin was outstanding in the way he marked John Toshack. He is the best young centre-half in the League. I don't think I would enjoy being a player-manager. It's a tough enough job without having to worry about trying to score the goals as well."

ALVIN MARTIN: "It was almost surreal finding myself up against John Toshack. It seems like only yesterday that I was standing on the terraces watching him play at Anfield when I was a schoolboy just dreaming of being a professional footballer. I was pleased with my performance, and now I think we have the confidence to give any of the remaining teams in the competition a difficult time. A lot of our football this season has been real quality."

THE MATCH FACTS

West Ham United 2, Swansea City 0

Half-time 0-0

Scorers: Paul Allen, David Cross (West Ham)

Attendance: 30,497

Teams:

WEST HAM UNITED	SWANSEA CITY
1 Phil Parkes	1 Glan Letheran
2 Frank Lampard	2 Neil Robinson
3 Paul Brush	3 David Rushbury
4 Ray Stewart	4 Leighton Phillips
5 Alvin Martin	5 Nigel Stevenson
6 Alan Devonshire	6 David Giles
7 Jimmy Neighbour	7 Tommy Craig
8 Stuart Pearson	8 Robbie James
9 David Cross	9 Jeremy Charles
10 Trevor Brooking	10 John Toshack
11 Geoff Pike	11 Ian Callaghan
12 Paul Allen	

Man of the match: David Cross

West Ham United 1, Aston Villa 0

NEVER had Ray Stewart's nerve and accuracy from the penalty spot been so severely tested as in this gripping FA Cup quarter-final against Aston Villa, watched by a sell-out capacity crowd at Upton Park.

There were just two minutes left and a replay in the Midlands was looking a stone-bonker certainty. But wait, what's this ... referee David Richardson had awarded the Hammers a penalty after Villa defender Ken McNaught, under pressure from David Cross, inexplicably handled the ball from a swinging Trevor Brooking corner.

Suddenly it was Ray Stewart versus battle-hardened Villa goalkeeper Jimmy Rimmer, a duel from twelve yards. One of the finest penalty experts in the League against a vastly experienced goalkeeper who had played superbly throughout the previous 87 minutes and had saved at least three certain goals.

As Stewart placed the ball on the penalty spot you could have heard a Cockney sparrer cough on the terraces. The 36,393 all-ticket crowd was as hushed as trappist monks with laryngitis.

The prize at stake, a ticket through to the FA Cup semi-final for West Ham, a replay and a survival chance for Aston Villa, who had been bombarded throughout the game by a Hammers team at the top of their game.

Stewart backed up, looked beyond Rimmer for where he was going to place the ball and then walked forward and struck his shot with thunderous power. Rimmer hardly had time to blink let alone move as the ball flashed by him into the net.

There was then an almighty eruption of sound as the West Ham fans celebrated not only one of the great penalty kicks but their team's progress through to the last four in the FA Cup – just ninety minutes from Wembley.

Not even the most biased Aston Villa supporter could deny that the Hammers thoroughly deserved their victory, narrow though it was on paper.

Everything was coming together beautifully for the Irons. They had moved up to a promotion challenging fifth place in the Second Division, and they had now proved they were ready for First Division status by clearly outplaying a team sitting in fifth place in the top table.

Apart from the Stewart penalty thunderbolt, this was a match that will always be remembered for the genius of Trevor Brooking. He played many exceptional games for the Hammers, but few better than this one against a Villa team that just could not read or restrain him.

Villa appeared to come in fear of the Hammers, and from the first minute set out their stall for a defensive policy as if manager Ron Saunders had decided that their best chance of reaching the semi-final was via a replay at Villa Park.

West Ham, with inspirational skipper Billy Bonds once again confined to the sidelines, mounted attack after attack, most of them instigated by Brooking, whose precise passes, fluent running and intelligent positional play continually put him a thought and a deed ahead of the Villa defenders. All it needed was for him to be handed a conductor's baton to show that he was orchestrating the entire performance.

Villa built a human barrier across their goal, defending in depth and usually in desperation. Jimmy Rimmer gave a performance on a par with the one by Phil Parkes against West Brom at the start of this Cup adventure.

His string of saves in the first-half included a blinder from a stinging shot by Brooking, who decided to try to find the net himself after his colleagues had spurned half a dozen chances that he had created.

David Cross and Stuart Pearson were like sportscars stuck in M25 traffic. They were not allowed any room in which to move by the disciplined and determined Villa defenders, and it was left to Geoff Pike and Alan Devonshire to come through from deep positions to try to turn Brooking's gliding geometry into goals.

You could almost feel the nervous tension rising on the terraces and invading the Chicken Run as the clock ticked down with no goals to show for all the territorial advantage.

Phil Parkes had been a spectator for most of the match but soon after the hour he had to move swiftly to cut out a shot from Gordon Cowans; then Brian Little scampered through to test him with a hard drive.

Villa had been pummelled from pillar to post, their defence dragged this way and that but they were still in the game, and West Ham did not have a single goal to show for all their attacking and the brilliance of Brooking.

Ten minutes to go and West Ham raised the pace yet again. Geoff Pike wormed his way through the Villa guard but was robbed of a goal by a suddenly raised hand by Rimmer, then an action replay after Paul Allen (on as substitute for injured Pearson), had forced his way into the packed penalty area.

Two minutes to go, and Brooking – it had to be Brooking – forced a corner on the left. He took it himself, sending the ball on a vicious swinging curve into the goalmouth. Alvin Martin, David Cross, Alan Devonshire – all West Ham's tall men – rose to try to meet the ball.

We looked on incredulously as the only thing that reached the ball was a hand. An Aston Villa hand. Ken McNaught's hand.

Penalty! And the rest is history … West Ham's football folklore in which Ray Stewart – the penalty king – will always feature.

Aston Villa goalkeeper Jimmy Rimmer, beaten by deadeye Ray Stewart in the penalty shoot-out duel

RAY STEWART: "This was when all my hours of shooting from the penalty spot at cones in training paid off. I held my nerve and just concentrated on placing the ball out of Jimmy Rimmer's reach. I don't think I have ever heard Upton Park as quiet as when I placed the ball on the spot. Then when the ball hit the back of the net you couldn't hear yourself think! I think it's fair to say I was relieved when the ball went in."

RON SAUNDERS: "Ken McNaught insists he did not handle the ball deliberately, but that it was headed against his hand by David Cross. There was such a melee of players there that I could not see exactly what happened. We had defended magnificently, and I am confident we would have won a replay at Villa Park where our tactics would have been completely different. I have wished John Lyall good luck. He has a very bright team, and if Trevor Brooking can maintain his form then they can go all the way. He was brilliant against us today, absolutely brilliant."

JOHN LYALL: "You not only have to admire Ray's accuracy from the penalty spot but also his nerve. I know many players in that situation would have muffed it because of the sheer tension of the occasion. There was so much riding on it, but Ray tucked it away as if he was in a training session. And how about Trevor today! He has developed into a true world-class player, and seems to improve with every match. Our first priority continues to be promotion, but it is impossible not to start thinking ahead to perhaps another FA Cup final at Wembley."

TREVOR BROOKING: "Villa allowed me a lot of space in which to work and I just got on and did my job. I thoroughly enjoyed the game, but I would have liked not to have had the anxiety caused by us not putting our chances away. It would have been an injustice if we had not won after having at least 70 per cent of the possession. When I fired our corner across I could not believe it when McNaught put his hand up and clearly deflected the ball. It seemed a very odd thing to do. And how about Ray's penalty. He is an absolute master from the spot, and nothing puts him off his stride. Another possible Wembley final around the corner. That would be nice …"

THE MATCH FACTS

West Ham United 1, Aston Villa 0
Half-time 0-0
Scorer: Ray Stewart, pen (West Ham)
Attendance: 36,393
Teams:

WEST HAM UNITED	ASTON VILLA
1 Phil Parkes	1 Jimmy Rimmer
2 Frank Lampard	2 Ivor Linton
3 Paul Brush	3 Colin Gibson
4 Ray Stewart	4 Brendan Ormsby
5 Alvin Martin	5 Ken McNaught
6 Alan Devonshire	6 Dennis Mortimer
7 Paul Allen	7 Des Bremner
8 Stuart Pearson	8 Brian Little
9 David Cross	9 Terry Donovan
10 Trevor Brooking	10 Gordon Cowans
11 Geoff Pike	11 Terry Bullivant

Man of the match: Trevor Brooking

West Ham United 1, Everton 1

THIS was not so much a semi-final as a 90-minute volcanic eruption. Rarely in their history have West Ham been involved in such a combative contest. There was an angrily disputed penalty, a sending-off, three bookings and a final frenzied 30 minutes during which Everton's ten men somehow held out against a West Ham team attacking on all fronts. Now they have to do it all again in four days' time at Leeds to decide which of them goes to Wembley in May for the first FA Cup final of the '80s.

The game had been hard, fair and even up until five minutes before half-time when Asa Hartford sent an innocuous-looking cross into the West Ham box. As Alan Devonshire jumped to head the ball clear, Everton forward Andy King went tumbling over. Did he dive or was he pushed? Referee Colin Seel decided the answer was that Devonshire had pushed him and pointed to the penalty spot.

Cue West Ham's players losing their rag, which is unusual for a club where they are always taught to accept the referee's decision. But this was an FA Cup semi-final, and the Hammers players were incensed. The referee was surrounded by West Ham protestors giving their version of the incident, and Devonshire and then Ray Stewart had their names taken for what the referee described as "showing dissent."

Bran Kidd, now into the veteran stage after long service with Man United, Arsenal and Man City, volunteered to take the spot-kick, and coolly fired the ball home low past the despairing dive of Phil Parkes.

The game became taut with tension and bad temper. Everton's Trevor Ross was booked for a reckless tackle on Stuart Pearson, and then somehow got away with just a lecture after scything down Trevor Brooking when the first gentleman of football was in full flight.

The game reached boiling point on the hour after a Stewart piledriver had knocked Trevor Ross out cold. Everton goalkeeper Martin Hodge hoofed the ball towards the touchline with Ross lying flat, and Kidd and Stewart became involved in an ugly scuffle as they chased after it.

After consulting a linesman, referee Seel decided that Kidd was the main culprit and sent him for an early bath. This brought the wrath of the Everton fans down on Mr. Seel, who was now the target for abuse from both sets of supporters.

West Ham equalised in the 70th minute with one of the crazier goals of the season. Brooking and Devonshire performed one of their magical one-two combinations and Trevor started motoring into the space they had opened up.

In the middle, just outside the penalty box, Stuart Pearson was picking himself up after a heavy tackle from Asa Hartford. He was hobbling and holding his shoulder in pain. As he saw Brooking making progress, he started to lurch into the penalty area like a drunk leaving a pub. Trevor found him with one of his immaculate passes and he suddenly straightened-up and hammered the ball into the net for an astonishing equaliser.

Moments later, goal hero Pearson hobbled off with a twisted knee, and his place was taken by substitute Geoff Pike. Only one substitute was allowed, so Patsy Holland – making his first Cup appearance of the season – had to carry on although in obvious pain because of a sprained ankle. Defenders Alvin Martin and Paul Brush (filling in for the injured Frank Lampard) were also showing signs of wear and tear in a game that had been fought at a furious pace throughout.

Everton, with survival now the name of their game, dropped back into deep and desperate defence. This was the signal for West Ham to push forward, with Devonshire and Brooking in joint charge of the demolition work.

But even with ten men, the Merseysiders were dangerous on the break and Phil Parkes deliberately stuck out one of his big legs to divert a Peter Eastoe shot. He later performed an identical save when Everton substitute Bob Latchford threatened to score. At the other end Hodge diverted a rocket shot from Ray Stewart and then saved a thumping header from the atomic Billy Bonds following a Brooking free-kick.

With the extra man, West Ham should have taken command but the magnitude of the occasion made them snatch at their shots and to lose their usual composure and control. The Cup was now their last chance of glory because they had slipped to ninth position in the Second Division race and promotion was beyond them.

Some of the Everton tackling in the second-half was close to criminal, but the referee continually turned a blind eye, possibly thinking that he might risk a lynching from Everton fans who were still pouring scorn on him for his decision to send off Kidd.

In the closing stages West Ham were playing with their foot hard down on the accelerator, when a more calm and collected approach might have paid greater dividends. Brooking and Devonshire were their usual poised and serene selves, but could not spread the tranquility to the players around them.

West Ham tempers briefly flared again when they had a penalty appeal turned down when John Gidman blatantly pulled Pike back by his shirt and, in the hectic closing moments, Paul Allen claimed a goal only to have it ruled off-side.

At the final whistle, players on both sides were in a state of extreme fatigue. The ten men of Everton had worked themselves into the ground, and West Ham had run themselves to the edge of exhaustion in an effort to collect a winning goal that would have rendered the trip to Elland Road for the replay unnecessary.

Stuart Pearson, the thinking man's striker who helped shoot West Ham to Wembley

ALAN DEVONSHIRE: "I never usually lose my rag on the football pitch, but I was hard done by. No way in a million years did I push King over. He backed into me as we both jumped for the ball, and he simply fell down. I don't think even he could believe it when the referee pointed to the penalty spot. If anything, it should have been a free-kick to us. I think we produced enough today to prove that we're every bit as good as Everton, and we can go into the replay at Elland Road with confidence."

STUART PEARSON: "I was waiting to call the trainer on for treatment when I noticed Trevor in possession and coming forward at a great rate of knots. I had pains in my knee and my shoulder, but I thought I should get into the box to try to make a nuisance of myself. Suddenly the ball was coming right to me with Trevor's typical accuracy and I just let fly. For a few seconds I forgot my pain as the ball hit the net, but I quickly realised that I could not play on. I just hope I can get fit for the replay, because I'm convinced we can make it to the final."

JOHN LYALL: "I think it fair to call that a competitive game! There was so much at stake that neither side would give an inch. Alan Devonshire is an honest lad, and he is adamant that he did not push King over. I don't condone the way he and several other of our players disputed the decision, but this was such an important game and a harsh penalty like that is enough to upset any player. Several of our players picked up knocks and it will be touch and go as to whether they will be fit for the replay. It will, to say the least, be interesting at Elland Road on Wednesday …!"

ANDY KING: "All I know is that I felt a shove in my back as I went up for the ball and I could not help but go over. I have never been a diver, and the referee had a good view of the incident. We felt hard done by when Brian Kidd was sent-off for what seemed to be a pushing and shoving affair with both players as guilty or as innocent as each other. It was six-of-one and half-a-dozen of the other. We know we are the better team and aim to prove it in the replay at Leeds. West Ham played above themselves and have yet to see us at our best."

THE MATCH FACTS

West Ham United 1, Everton 1
Half-time 0-1
Scorers: Stuart Pearson (West Ham)
Brian Kidd, pen (Everton)
Attendance: 47,685
Teams:

WEST HAM UNITED

1 Phil Parkes
2 Ray Stewart
3 Paul Brush
4 Billy Bonds
5 Alvin Martin
6 Alan Devonshire
7 Paul Allen
8 Stuart Pearson
9 David Cross
10 Trevor Brooking
11 Pat Holland
12 Geoff Pike

EVERTON

1 Martin Hodge
2 John Gidman
3 John Bailey
4 Billy Wright
5 Mick Lyons
6 Peter Eastoe
7 Gary Megson
8 Andy King
9 Brian Kidd
10 Asa Hartford
11 Trevor Ross
12 Bob Latchford

Man of the match: Billy Bonds

West Ham United 2, Everton 1

ALL the goals came in extra-time in an epic and emotional semi-final that West Ham used as a springboard to their third post-war FA Cup final at Wembley. The fact that the winning goal was scored with a diving header from veteran full-back Frank Lampard added to the drama of a memorable match.

Everton were again muscular, West Ham almost musical – with the 'Terrible Twins' Trevor Brooking and Alan Devonshire setting the tempo and the orchestrations.

Playing at the Elland Road ground where Leeds United built their reputation for dishing out bruising punishment, Everton seemed to have convinced themselves that the way to beat the 'southern softies' of West Ham was to make the game a physical rather than football challenge.

Wrong! West Ham matched them in the physical department – particularly at the centre of their defence, where Ray Stewart and Billy Bonds were heroic in a partnership forced on them by an injury to Alvin Martin.

And when it came to the footballing department, West Ham were a country mile better than the Merseysiders with classic, free-flowing movements that gave Everton a lesson in how the game could and should be played.

The Goodison club have a fine footballing pedigree of their own, and for neutrals it was sad to see them putting brute force and strength ahead of flair and skill. Perhaps it has been their season-long fight against relegation from the First Division that has drained Everton of confidence, but they might have had a better chance of taming the Hammers had they played with the old Everton style and swagger.

This was the night that Alan Devonshire, the former Hoover-employed forklift truck driver, showed that he stands comparison with the best midfield players in the land. He floated almost nonchalantly around the pitch, ghosting past the Everton attempts to kick him into the Elland Road stands. Whether running with the ball in the graceful, head-held-high style of his – or passing it with pin-pointed accuracy – he was the star of the show, even out-glittering the poised and polished Trevor Brooking.

After a deadlocked 90 minutes, it was Devonshire's gem of a goal that lit up the game like a meteor in the night sky.

Extra-time was four minutes old when the player who had been troubling Everton all night combined first with Trevor Brooking and then David Cross, accepting their instant passes and then nutmegging Everton defender Billy Wright before sweeping the ball past goalkeeper Martin Hodge. It was a Brazilian-style goal scored on English grass and show-cased the skill that comes naturally and delightfully to the elusive, elegant Devonshire.

It looked good enough to win a game in which both teams were almost out on their feet following the 90-minute slog to extra-time and the sometimes brutal battle at Villa Park four days earlier.

The Wembley final was just seven minutes away when Bob Latchford struck a shock equaliser for Everton. Wright cut deep into the West Ham defence and sent over a low pass that Latchford met at the near post and glanced it past the desolate Parkes.

It seemed odds-on a second replay when – with just two minutes to go – a Devonshire/Brooking-inspired attack culminated with the ball being pushed across goal by David Cross, and there – diving forward like a kid on a trampoline – was the 'old boy' Frank Lampard, turning almost sideways as he twisted to meet the ball with his head and guide it over the line for one of the most important goals in West Ham history. It was the most magical moment of Frank's sixteen years as a Hammers player, and he celebrated by skipping crazily around the corner flag like a demonic pole dancer.

Everton players, who had given their all, sank to the ground at the final whistle like bayoneted soldiers, while the West Ham team and their supporters celebrated with the sort of Cockney knees-up exclusive to the Hammers. Rarely has Mrs Brown had such eager demands to bring her knees up.

On a count back of chances created over the full 120 minutes, West Ham thoroughly deserved their victory. Everton were too often relying on raw power, while West Ham were purring along, making the ball do the work and conserving their energy for the moves that really mattered. Phil Parkes saved brilliantly from Trevor Ross during Everton's best moments in the opening 30 minutes and, early in the second-half, Bonds headed in off a post from a beautifully flighted Brooking free-kick, bit it was ruled out because the referee spotted a push in the penalty area just before Billy netted.

What pleased the purists is that West Ham's win was a victory for football. Everton, traditionally a club putting skill before steel, chose to play a physically intimidating game and came unstuck. They underestimated the size of the hearts beating inside the claret and blue shirts, and failed to realise that the players were ready to run through brick walls for that prized place at Wembley.

In Billy Bonds and Ray Stewart, Everton came up against two tough characters who could give as good as they got in the strongarm stuff, while around them players like Devonshire and Brooking were playing stunning off-the-cuff football that was not only good to watch but penetrating and, eventually, match-winning. They also had youngsters like Paul Allen and Geoff Pike who could run all day, and with an enthusiasm and an energy that rubbed off on the players around them.

West Ham had done their job and booked their place at Wembley.

Now they had to wait to see who they would be playing in the final.

Frank Lampard, the West Ham loyalist who scored one of the most vital goals in the club's history

JOHN LYALL: "Mission accomplished! I don't mind confessing I was very worried when it was clear Alvin Martin was not going to be fit for the replay, but Ray Stewart and Billy Bonds were just magnificent together. I think tonight Alan Devonshire made a lot of people sit up and take notice of him. He would not be out of place in an England shirt. He monopolised in midfield and his brilliant goal was the icing on the cake. We are all thrilled for Frank Lampard. He is West Ham through and through and his winning goal could not have happened for a more deserving player. Whether we face Liverpool or Arsenal in the final, we will be ready for them. We have already shown we have no reason to fear any team."

ALAN DEVONSHIRE: "I am still pinching myself to make sure this is all really happening and not a dream. It was only four years ago that I was playing in front of a few hundred spectators as a part-time pro with Southall and driving a forklift truck for my living. Now it's going to be 100,000 spectators at Wembley in the FA Cup final. I was a bit pleased with my goal, and I would like to thank Trevor and David for the part they played in helping create it."

BOB LATCHFORD: "When I scored the equaliser I was convinced I had earned us another replay. But you have to give West Ham credit for the way they picked themselves up and managed to snatch the winner that was a real killer goal for us. Don't write West Ham off in the final whoever they play. They may be down in the Second Division, but the football they play is First Division standard."

FRANK LAMPARD: "When I dived for the ball it was more in hope than anything. The ball could have gone anywhere, and I was over the moon to see it going into the net. I went a bit potty and found myself dancing round the corner flag! I've played in several outstanding West Ham teams and this one's as good as any of them. We have the right balance, a great team spirit and more skill than most First Division teams. Liverpool or Arsenal in the final? We don't care. Our confidence is so high we think we could beat either of them. We won't start favourites, but that never bothers us."

THE MATCH FACTS

West Ham United 2, Everton 1 (after extra-time)
Half-time 0-0, Full-time 0-0
Scorers: Alan Devonshire, Frank Lampard (West Ham)
Bob Latchford (Everton)
Attendance: 40,720
Teams:

WEST HAM UNITED	EVERTON
1 Phil Parkes	1 Martin Hodge
2 Frank Lampard	2 John Gidman
3 Paul Brush	3 John Bailey
4 Ray Stewart	4 Billy Wright
5 Billy Bonds	5 Mick Lyons
6 Alan Devonshire	6 Kevin Ratcliffe
7 Paul Allen	7 Andy King
8 Stuart Pearson	8 Peter Eastoe
9 David Cross	9 Bob Latchford
10 Trevor Brooking	10 Asa Hartford
11 Geoff Pike	11 Trevor Ross
	12 Imre Varadi

Man of the match: Alan Devonshire

THE OPPONENTS: *ARSENAL*

WEST HAM had to wait until just nine days before the final to discover they would be meeting Cup-holders Arsenal at Wembley. The Gunners got locked in a four-match semi-final marathon with Liverpool that set a long-playing record, eventually reaching their third successive final thanks to a 1-0 victory at Coventry's Highfield Road stadium.

Arsenal had been chasing trophies on four fronts, going out of the League Cup in the quarter-finals and finishing fourth in the First Division title race (Liverpool retained the championship two days after their FA Cup semi-final exit). The North Londoners were scheduled to meet Valencia in the European Cup Winners' Cup final four days after defending the FA Cup against the Hammers at Wembley.

In a season in which they played a demanding 70 matches, Arsenal had got themselves into a fixture backlog and were fighting fatigue in the hectic closing weeks. Manager Terry Neill admitted: "We are nearing exhaustion point, but success is the best possible antidote to tiredness. Let's face it, we would rather be involved in finals than resting at home watching the games on television. Being heavily occupied in the business end of things is what it's all about."

It was the third successive year that Neill would be leading out an Arsenal team in an FA Cup final. They were shocked to defeat by Ipswich in 1978 and won a dramatic match against Manchester United in 1979. Alan Sunderland scored a late winner to give the Gunners a 3-2 victory over Manchester United, three goals coming in the last five breathtaking minutes.

The Gunners survived a scare in their opening third round match as they set out in defence of the trophy, scrambling a goalless draw at Cardiff before winning the replay 2-1 at Highbury. A double strike by 1979 hero Alan Sunderland put them through.

In the fourth round they won 2-0 in a home tie against First Division strugglers Brighton, and then got involved in another replay after a 1-1 fifth round draw at Bolton. Sunderland again scored twice as Arsenal won the replay 3-0.

The red and whites made the short trip to Watford for a 2-1 sixth round victory, Frank Stapleton netting the two goals.

They then got bogged down in a four-match semi-final serial with Liverpool, before a Brian Talbot goal settled it in favour of the North Londoners in the third replay at Coventry. A total of 179,163 spectators saw the four matches, and they paid a then record £620,037 in gate receipts.

HOW THE GUNNERS GOT TO WEMBLEY

THIRD ROUND: Saturday January 5, Ninian Park. Attendance: 21,972
Cardiff City 0, Arsenal 0
Jennings, Devine, Rice (c), Talbot, Walford, Young, Gatting, Sunderland, Stapleton, Hollins, Rix.

THIRD ROUND REPLAY: Tuesday January 8, Highbury. Attendance: 36,582
Arsenal 2, Cardiff City 1
Scorers: Sunderland (2) (Arsenal); Buchanan (Cardiff)
Jennings, Rice (c), Nelson, Talbot, Walford, Young, Gatting, Sunderland, Stapleton, Hollins, Rix.

FOURTH ROUND: Saturday January 26, Highbury. Attendance: 43,202
Arsenal 2, Brighton & Hove Albion 0
Scorers: Nelson, Talbot (Arsenal)
Jennings, Rice (c), Nelson, Talbot, O'Leary, Young, Brady, Sunderland, Stapleton, Price, Rix.

FIFTH ROUND: Saturday February 16, Burnden Park. Attendance: 32,530
Bolton Wanderers 1, Arsenal 1
Scorers: Stapleton (Arsenal); Allardyce (Bolton)
Jennings, Rice (c), Nelson, Talbot, O'Leary, Young, Brady, Sunderland, Stapleton, Price, Rix.

FIFTH ROUND REPLAY: Tuesday February 19, Highbury. Attendance: 40,614
Arsenal 3, Bolton Wanderers 0
Scorers: Sunderland (2), Stapleton (Arsenal)
Jennings, Rice (c), Nelson, Talbot, O'Leary, Young, Brady, Sunderland, Stapleton, Price, Rix.

QUARTER-FINAL: Saturday March 8, Vicarage Road. Attendance: 28,000
Watford 1, Arsenal 2
Scorers: Stapleton (2) (Arsenal); Poskett (Watford)
Jennings, Devine, Nelson, Talbot, O'Leary, Young, Brady, Sunderland (Gatting), Stapleton, Price, Rix.

SEMI-FINAL: Saturday April 12, Hillsborough. Attendance: 50,174
Arsenal 0, Liverpool 0
Jennings, Rice (c), Nelson (Walford), Talbot, O'Leary, Young, Brady, Sunderland, Stapleton, Price, Rix.

SEMI-FINAL REPLAY: Wednesday April 16, Villa Park. Attendance: 40,679
Arsenal 1, Liverpool 1 (aet)
Scorers: Sunderland (Arsenal); Fairclough (Liverpool)
Jennings, Rice (c), Walford, Talbot, O'Leary, Young, Brady, Sunderland, Stapleton, Price, Rix.

SEMI-FINAL SECOND REPLAY: Monday April 28, Villa Park. Attendance: 42,975
Arsenal 1, Liverpool 1 (aet)
Scorers: Sunderland (Arsenal); Dalglish (Liverpool)
Jennings, Rice (c), Devine, Talbot, O'Leary, Young, Brady, Sunderland, Stapleton, Price, Rix.

SEMI-FINAL THIRD REPLAY: Thursday May 1, Highfield Road. Attendance: 35,335
Arsenal 1, Liverpool 0
Scorer: Talbot (Arsenal)
Jennings, Rice (c), Devine, Talbot, O'Leary, Young, Brady, Sunderland, Stapleton, Price, Rix.

THE ARSENAL PLAYERS

MANAGER Terry Neill called on 20 players during the Arsenal chase for four trophies. The only regular choice who missed out on the FA Cup final was John Hollins, who had arrived from Queens Park Rangers in the summer of 1979. He made 23 League appearances plus he came off the substitute's bench three times. These were the tried and tested Arsenal players West Ham would be meeting at Wembley:

1 PAT JENNINGS
Goalkeeper. Born Newry, Northern Ireland, June 12 1945. 6ft 12st 8lbs
Clubs: Watford, Tottenham, Arsenal
Northern Ireland international: 119 caps

Arguably the finest British goalkeeper of all time, the hefty cruiserweight of an Irishman was into his third season with Arsenal after being surprisingly let go by Tottenham, where he achieved legendary status. With hands like huge pink shovels and a heart the size of a cabbage, Pat did not have a single weakness in his game. He was a perfectionist with his positioning, had cat-like reflexes, caught the ball comfortably and could stretch himself across goal like an Olympic gymnast. He was into the veteran stage and played his 119th and last game for Northern Ireland on his 41st birthday during the 1982 World Cup finals.

2 PAT RICE
Right-back. Born Belfast, March 17 1949. 5ft 8in, 11st 4lbs
Clubs: Arsenal, Watford
Northern Ireland international: 49 caps

Captain and right-back, Pat was the sole survivor from the Arsenal team that won the League and FA Cup double in 1970-71. Belfast-born but London raised, he was capped 49 times by Northern Ireland and at the end of this 1979-80 season he moved to Watford with whom he made a sixth Cup final appearance against Everton in 1984. Returned to Arsenal as a youth team coach, then right-hand man to first George Graham and later Arsene Wenger. A fierce and determined defender, unflappable Pat was a master of overlapping play and a careful rather than creative distributor of the ball out of defence.

Pat Jennings, the genius of a goalkeeper who spurred Arsenal to new heights

3 JOHN DEVINE

Left-back. Born Dublin November 11 1958. 5ft 10in 12st 4lbs
Clubs: Arsenal, Norwich, Stoke City, IK Start, Shamrock Rovers
Republic of Ireland international: 13 caps

Happiest at right-back, he played in the No 3 shirt against West Ham. He took over from Pat Rice at No 2 the following season for the peak moments of a career that was cruelly curtailed by a badly broken leg. John won 13 Republic of Ireland caps, and would have collected many more but for the injury. He spent much of his time at Highbury understudying full-back partners Rice and Sammy Nelson, occasionally getting into the League team as a holding midfield player. John had a solid tackle and was a disciplined and determined marker. He later played fleetingly for Norwich, Stoke, IK Start in Norway and Shamrock Rovers before becoming a respected coach.

4 BRIAN TALBOT

Right midfield. Born Ipswich July 21 1953. 5ft 10in 12st 1lb
Clubs: Ipswich Town, Arsenal, Watford, Stoke City, WBA, Fulham, Aldershot
England international: 6 caps

Brian had been a winner at Wembley in the two previous FA Cup finals, first for his original club Ipswich against Arsenal in 1978 and then for the Gunners against Manchester United a year later. An ever-present in all Arsenal's 70 matches in 1979-80, the marathon running midfielder scored the goal that finally ended Liverpool's interest in the FA Cup in the drawn-out semi-final saga. Capped six times by England, Brian plundered 40 goals in 254 League games for the Gunners before later playing for Watford, Stoke, West Brom, Fulham and Aldershot. He went into management, including being boss at West Brom, Hibs, Rushden & Diamonds, Oldham and Oxford United.

5 DAVID O'LEARY

Central defender. Born Stoke Newington May 2 1958. 5ft 11in 11st 5lbs
Clubs: Arsenal, Leeds United. Republic of Ireland international: 68 caps, 1 goal

Highbury loyalist David made a club record 722 first-team appearances over a span of 18 years from 1975, and was a steadying influence on a procession of Arsenal teams. Nicknamed 'Spider' because of his long legs, he was equally comfortable in the centre of the defence or playing as a midfield anchorman. Commanding in the air, he was a footballing defender always on the look out to turn defence into attack. He was a fixture in the Republic of Ireland team, winning 68 caps. David wound down his playing career with Leeds, the club he later managed before a stint in charge of Aston Villa. He has recently been managing Al-Ahli Dubai in the United Arab Emirates.

6 WILLIE YOUNG

Central defender. Born Edinburgh November 25 1951. 6ft 3in, 12st 12lbs
Clubs: Aberdeen, Spurs, Arsenal, Nottingham Forest, Norwich, Brighton, Darlington

Like Pat Jennings, Willie made the 'forbidden' move across North London from Tottenham to Arsenal in 1977. Strong in the air and an uncompromising defender, he formed a powerful partnership with David O'Leary at the heart of the Gunners defence. He laid the foundation to his career with Aberdeen, and would have won a stack of Scotland caps but for getting himself banned for life following an incident in a Danish nightclub while on an international tour. After four years with the Gunners, he later played for Nottingham Forest, Norwich, Brighton and Darlington until recurring injuries forced his retirement in 1984 at the age of 32.

7 LIAM BRADY

Midfield schemer. Born Dublin February 13 1956. 5ft 7in, 10st 9lbs
Clubs: Arsenal, Juventus, Sampdoria, Inter Milan, Ascoli, West Ham
Republic of Ireland international: 72 caps, 9 goals

Known either as 'Chippy' or 'The Claw', Liam was the scheming genius who made Arsenal tick. He had a left foot that could open safe doors, and an instinctive feel for where to be and when to make himself available for passes before delivering the ball on a sixpence to unmarked team-mates. He took his bag of tricks to Italy after the 1980 FA Cup final and performed elegantly for Juventus, Sampdoria, Inter and Ascoli before returning to England to play out his career with the Hammers from 1987 until 1990. He dabbled with management with Celtic and Brighton and then went 'home' to Arsenal and became head of youth development. He won 72 Republic of Ireland caps.

8 ALAN SUNDERLAND

Support striker. Born Conisbrough, Yorkshire July 1 1953. 5ft 9in, 11st 7lbs
Clubs: Wolves, Arsenal, Ipswich Town. England international: 1 cap

Famous for his bubble-perm and Wembley goal celebration, midfielder-turned-striker Alan was the Arsenal hero with the match-winner against Manchester United in the 'five-minute final' of 1979. He got a good grounding to his career with Wolves before joining Arsenal as a midfield player in 1977 and then pushing forward in the role of support striker. He scored 55 goals in 206 League games for the Gunners before finishing his career with Ipswich. Alan, who won a solitary England cap against Australia, became a publican in Ipswich before retiring to Malta where he has been involved in coaching local teams.

Frank Stapleton, a goal striker idolised at Highbury and Old Trafford

9 FRANK STAPLETON

Centre-forward. Born Dublin July 10 1956. 6ft 12st 8lbs

Clubs: Arsenal, Man United, Ajax, Anderlecht, Derby, Le Havre, Blackburn, Aldershot, Huddersfield, Bradford, Brighton. Republic of Ireland international: 71 caps, 20 goals

A powerhouse of a centre-forward, Frank had a potent partnership with the more subtle Alan Sunderland and played in all three of Arsenal's Cup finals from 1978 to 1980. He banged in 75 goals in 225 League games for the Gunners before demanding a move to Manchester United against the wishes of Arsenal. In six years at Old Trafford he scored 60 goals in 223 League matches. Frank was also a prolific marksman for the Republic of Ireland, netting 20 goals in 71 internationals. He later took his shooting boots to Ajax, Anderlecht, Blackburn, Aldershot, Huddersfield, Bradford and Brighton, and managed Bradford City and New England Revolution.

10 DAVID PRICE

Midfielder. Born Caterham, Surrey June 23 1955. 5ft 11in 12st 2lbs
Clubs: Arsenal, Peterborough (loan), Crystal Palace, Orient

A former captain of England schoolboys, David was a hot Highbury prospect who did not quite live up to his promise – mainly because of injuries that forced his premature retirement at 28 after he had moved down the soccer chain with Crystal Palace and then Orient. At his peak with Arsenal, he played in the three successive FA Cup finals but eventually lost his place when John Hollins arrived from Queens Park Rangers. A hard-working midfield water carrier, he made 176 appearances for the Gunners between 1970 and 1981 before moving to Selhurst Park. After his early retirement, he became a taxi driver in Croydon.

11 GRAHAM RIX

Left midfield. Born Askern, South Yorkshire October 23 1957. 5ft 9in 11st 2lbs.
Clubs: Arsenal, Brentford (loan), Caen, Le Havre, Dundee, Chelsea
England international: 17 caps

He patrolled in midfield with Liam Brady, and was almost in the class of 'Chippy' with his left foot. His skill earned him 17 England caps, and in 351 League games for the Gunners he netted 41 goals. In 1983 he became captain of the club he had joined as an apprentice in 1974, but failed to collect any silverware. He later played for Brentford, Caen, Le Havre, Dundee and had just one game for Chelsea when assistant manager to Glenn Hoddle. He enjoyed little success when in charge of Portsmouth, Oxford and Hearts, and became a coach at Hoddle's soccer academy in Spain following headline-hitting personal problems.

12 SAMMY NELSON

Substitute, defender. Born Belfast April 1 1949. 5ft 10in 11st 0lbs
Clubs: Arsenal, Brighton & Hove Albion. Northern Ireland international: 51 caps

A winger when he first joined Arsenal in 1966, he was converted to left-back and played 255 League games for the Gunners during his fifteen years at Highbury. He succeeded Bob McNab as the regular No 3, and was noted for his speed, ball control, tackling and whole-hearted effort. Sammy was capped 51 times in various defensive roles for Northern Ireland. He joined Brighton in 1981 and helped them reach the FA Cup final in his last season in the game before briefly becoming a coach with the Albion. Sammy then sold insurance, and later worked as a tour guide at the Emirates Stadium that was built long after he had left Highbury.

FINAL COUNTDOWN: *The Captains' Table*

DURING the last week countdown to the FA Cup final, Norman Giller was assigned to put questions to each of the rival captains – Pat Rice and Billy Bonds – for the late, lamented London *Evening News*. These were the questions and the replies:

Pat, you must be exhausted after that four-match semi-final slog with Liverpool. Do you have the energy left for Saturday's final?

'It is all about attitude of mind now. We have the incentive to win not one but two trophies in these last few days of the season, and that keeps the thoughts of tiredness away. There will be plenty of time to recharge our batteries once the Cup Winners' Cup final is out of the way. But for now, all our concentration is on Saturday's FA Cup final against West Ham. The win against Liverpool has given us a terrific lift. You only feel exhausted when you lose!'

Billy, Second Division against First Division. Can you close the quality gap against an all-international Arsenal side?

'Ask West Brom. Ask Aston Villa. Ask Everton. We feel we are First Division in everything but name. Our priority this season was to get promotion to the First Division, but now we are looking to the FA Cup to bring us consolation and to give our fantastic supporters the trophy they deserve. We think that when it comes to playing quality football, we can match any side in the country and that includes the Arsenal. There is no gap between us.'

Pat, this is your third final in three successive years. Is there a risk of a 'here we go again' complacency creeping in?

'Far from it. Our experience in the last two finals has taught us that the game has to have our full focus. Against Ipswich, everybody was tipping an easy victory for us, and the pain of that defeat still hurts. I don't want to go through it ever again. Then in the match with Manchester United last season we thought we were coasting to a comfortable win when United scored those two late goals. I have never known the sort of euphoria that greeted Alan Sunderland's winner. It was the craziest five minutes of football with which I've ever been involved.'

Billy, how does this West Ham team rate with the one you led to the 2-0 victory victory against Fulham in the 1975 FA Cup final?

'I have no hesitation in saying this is the best West Ham team that I've had the privilege of skippering. Anybody who has watched us on a regular basis this season will confirm that some of our football has been out of this world. The performances in particular of Trevor Brooking and Alan Devonshire have been pure class, and there is not a goalkeeper in the entire League who is in better form than big Phil Parkes. He played West Brom on his own in our first tie, and I told him afterwards that after a performance like that our name must be on the FA Cup.'

Pat, in your fellow-Irishman Pat Jennings you have one of the world's greatest goalkeepers. What does he bring to your defence?

'In a word, confidence. To know that you have a goalkeeper of Pat's ability behind you gives the whole team a lift. I have played with him for years at international level, and I have never known anybody match him for command of his goal area. I had just started as an apprentice at Highbury when Pat made his international debut in the same match as George Best, and I have watched him closely ever since and am so proud that he is a countryman. He is an outstanding ambassador for the game, a true sportsman and simply the best.'

Billy, if you had to pick one highlight from your run to Wembley what would it be?

'Apart from Parksie's goalkeeping display in the third round against West Brom, it has to be Frank Lampard's winning goal against Everton in the semi-final replay. It was his only goal of the season, and what a time and in what a match to get it. We were still getting over the choker of Everton snatching an equaliser and thinking that we were going to a second replay when Frank dived in to score. The Everton players could not believe it. And, to be honest, I'm not sure we could either! We were all thrilled for Frank who has been such a loyal club man.'

Pat, if you had to pick one highlight from your run to Wembley what would it be?

'It can only be hearing the final whistle to signal our win over Liverpool in the third replay! Brian Talbot had scored an early goal, and we slogged away trying to hang on to it. If Liverpool had forced another replay I don't know what we would have done with our outstanding fixtures. We are still way behind with our games. The FA were trying to get us to agree to a penalty shoot-out to decide the winners if it had gone to another replay, but our chairman Denis Hill-Wood said he would never ever agree to that. Thank goodness we settled it without a lottery. '

Billy, the rumour is that John Lyall is going to play 17-year-old Paul Allen. Is this a gamble?

'Paul is a brilliant young player with an old head on his shoulders. He has been outstanding with us all season, and playing like a seasoned professional. I would not see it as a gamble if he plays, but a good selection. He comes from a family that is steeped in football and will have been dreaming of a chance like this since he first kicked a ball. For somebody so young, he has a remarkable understanding of tactics, and always manages to get in the right positions. He is one of several marvellous youngsters in our squad, and we have confidence in each one of them.'

Brian Talbot, the midfield marathon man whose goal settled the semi-final stalemate

Pat, if you were in Terry Neill's shoes what would be your advice to the team just before they leave the dressing-room?

'Terry has got enough words of his own without me trying to put more into his mouth! But what I would say is that we've worked bloody hard to get here and now we must not throw it all away by giving a below-par performance. Keep focused, keep tight on them particularly in midfield and play as if we are up against the greatest team in the world. On no account must we underestimate West Ham. They have proved they deserve to be in the final, but we must not give them a second to settle and think they are anything like as good as us.'

Billy, if you were in John Lyall's shoes what would be your advice to the team just before they leave the dressing-room?

'I am sure that John will tell us that our job is not yet done. We must not look at reaching the final as the end of our mission. Our target has to be to win the game against a side that must surely be physically drained after their semi-final marathon against Liverpool. We will be the underdogs but by working hard for each other and keeping composed we can cause an upset. Arsenal are an exceptional team but we must not show them too much respect. We can match them for skill all over the pitch, and can win the game by being more industrious than them.'

FINAL COUNTDOWN: *The Managers*

D URING the last week countdown to the final, Norman Giller was assigned to put questions to each of the rival managers – Terry Neill and John Lyall – for the late, lamented London *Evening News*. These were the questions and the replies:

Terry, how are you going to motivate your players after the marathon FA Cup semi-final saga with Liverpool?

'Just the magical words 'Wembley, FA Cup final' are motivation enough. I'll not pretend we are not feeling the effect of the fixture pile-up, and we're extremely disappointed that the Football League have not been more considerate in helping us with our backlog of games. But we are professionals and will just get on with the job in hand. We've been adopting a take-each-game-as-it-comes policy for several months now. Saturday it's the FA Cup final. Our full concentration will be on that, and then we will switch our attention to the European Cup Winners' Cup final. One game at a time.'

John, how are you going to lift your players for what looks on paper a very daunting task?

'The fact that this is Wembley and the FA Cup final could not be a bigger lift. It's the game every player dreams about from the first moment he starts kicking the ball as a kid. My job is not so much lifting the players as instilling in them the belief that they can win, while all the experts are writing us off. I have been reminding them of the finals of 1973 when Sunderland beat Leeds, 1976 when Southampton beat Man United and in particular 1978 when Ipswich beat Arsenal. We have nothing to lose, and I would say all the pressure is on Arsenal. We are looking forward to a nice day out!'

Terry, what have you learned from your last two FA Cup finals that will help with this one against West Ham?

'Not to lose as we did against Ipswich, and not to give ourselves heart failure in the last few minutes, as we did against Man United. Seriously, we have known the best of times and the worst of times in our last two visits to Wembley, and I can assure you that the best of times is a much better experience. We will be very careful not to underestimate West Ham. They are an excellent football team, and we are not going to be fooled by that label they carry of being a Second Division side. They are without question First Division quality, we will will be giving them the respect they deserve.'

John, you last led West Ham out at Wembley in 1975 when you beat Fulham. What is the difference in the team from then?

'The major difference is that the '75 team was one largely built by Ron Greenwood, while this is very much MY team. There are just three survivors from that 1975 side, Frank Lampard, Billy Bonds and Trevor Brooking. I can say without hesitation that this is a stronger team. Our goalkeeper Phil Parkes is world-class, and I cannot think of two midfield players in the entire League who can match Brooking and Alan Devonshire for skill and invention. We have a good work ethic, and team spirit is as good as I've ever known at the club. Everybody is willing to work for everybody else. We do not have prima donnas. It is a team of which I am very proud.'

Liam 'Chippy' Brady, Arsenal's midfield marshal with the magical left foot

FINAL COUNTDOWN: *The Managers*

Terry, what plans have you got to control Trevor Brooking and Alan Devonshire who have been getting rave reports throughout West Ham's Cup run?

'That would be telling! Don Howe and I have carefully monitored West Ham and we know their strengths and weaknesses. There is no doubt that Brooking and Devonshire have been in outstanding form, but you can take it that we will not be giving them the freedom of Wembley. I prefer to think of our midfield players like Liam Brady, Graham Rix and Brian Talbot. It is West Ham who will have their hands full trying to control them. A lot has been made of our semi-final serial, but don't forget that it was against Liverpool who have just retained the League title. And we beat them.'

John, what plans have you got to control Liam Brady, Graham Rix and Brian Talbot who have been in exceptional form during Arsenal's Cup run?

'This is not the place to be discussing our tactics. I will save that for our team meetings. Suffice to say that I have a plan that will come as a surprise to everybody. You don't have to be Einstein to realise this match is going to be won and lost in midfield, where both sides are very strong. If you do a player-by-player breakdown of the two teams you will find there is not that much between us to justify the sort of nonsense being written. To read some of the articles, you would think all Arsenal have to do to win is turn up. No guarantees, but we have a plan that could lead to yet another Wembley upset.'

FINAL COUNTDOWN: *The Managers*

Terry, most of your team will have played 70 games by the time the season ends, not counting their international matches. Don't you worry about the burn-out factor?

'I would be more worried if we had played only 60 matches and finished up out of the hunt for all the major prizes. This has been a fantastic season for us. We have been in the hunt for the four major trophies, and still have a chance of picking up two of them. We were desperately disappointed to miss out on the League championship, but we will set our sights on it again next season. As for there being too much football, that is another argument altogether and one that I am sure will be addressed in the coming months. Is there anybody brave enough to say that 22 clubs in the First Division is at least two too many?'

John, there is a strong rumour that you're going to make 17-year-old Paul Allen the youngest ever Wembley finalist. Can you confirm it?

'I won't be confirming my team until just before the game, but let me just say that I would have no concerns about naming Paul in the side. He has had an excellent first season in senior football and plays with a maturity beyond his years. Paul is a wonderful advertisement for our youth academy and is one of several home-grown players who I know would represent us well at Wembley. I am a great believer in the old football saying, 'if you're good enough, you're old enough.' Young Paul definitely comes into that category.'

Gun to your head time, Terry. What do you expect the outcome to be on Saturday?

❝Well I cannot preach being positive to my players unless I am also positive, so I am going to predict a close, entertaining game with Arsenal coming out on top with a one or two goal advantage. I had similar feelings before the final against Ipswich two years ago, and we know what happened there. But that defeat has served us well. We never go into a major match with even a hint of complacency, and it will be no different against West Ham. We will ignore the fact that they play in the Second Division. They have some top-notch players and a manager who is a very good tactician. But I am confident that we will get the better of them.❞

Gun to your head time, John. What do you expect the outcome to be on Saturday?

❝I have been in the game too long to be drawn into making predictions. What I will say is that we are quietly confident that we can prove the experts wrong. As you will discover on Saturday, I have a plan that will surprise a lot of people. If it goes as I see it in my head, then we could be doing exactly what Ipswich did two years ago when they beat Arsenal after being dismissed as having no chance. With so many fine controllers of the ball on the pitch, I am sure it is going to be a good game to watch and I selfishly hope that Arsenal are going to find that their semi-final marathon against Liverpool catches up with them.❞

 **FINAL COUNTDOWN**: *West Ham Go to the Dogs*

JOHN LYALL was determined to keep a relaxed, pressure-off approach to the final, and on the eve of the match the West Ham players went *en masse* from their Middlesex hotel to Wembley greyhound track. Phil Parkes handed Alan Devonshire a tenner to put on a dog of his choice. It romped in at 4-1, and when Devs gave Parksie his £40 they saw it as a good omen and it put them in a winning mood (this, remember, when 40 quid was more than Devs had earned in a week while driving a forklift truck for a living).

Earlier in the day John had told the players the team. Paul Allen WAS in, and at 17 years 256 days he would become the youngest player ever to appear in an FA Cup final at Wembley.

The Hammers boss was relieved to also be able to select skipper Billy Bonds, who had been sweating on a hearing at the Football Association over his disciplinary record. He had collected 20 points, including three for being sent-off after a scuffle with Birmingham defender Colin Todd at Upton Park just three weeks before the final.

Bonzo was let-off with a fine and a severe talking to about his aggressive style of play. Billy politely and wisely nodded his agreement as he was instructed to be less combative in future, while secretly deciding to continue playing his normal game. To take the aggression away from Bonzo would be like pulling the teeth of a lion. He knew only one way to play the game, and that was with a fiercely competitive spirit – hard but fair. West Ham's ethos was all about fair play, and Billy would not have got near the team had he been a deliberately dirty player. He believed in playing a man's game like a man.

Lyall's hardest job was having to tell Paul Brush that he would be relegated to substitute. "That was very difficult for me," John confided later. "Paul had done a magnificent job for us throughout the Cup run, covering for both full-backs and performing any job I asked of him. But I fielded the team that I thought was best equipped to carry out my plan and that meant I wanted a back line of Ray Stewart, Billy Bonds, Alvin Martin and Frank Lampard. Paul took my decision like a man, and was still an important part of the team although wearing the number twelve shirt."

For one of the few times, John was able to name what he considered his strongest side, which meant he was able to spring his carefully planned trap designed to stifle an Arsenal team that was odds-on to win the match.

While the West Ham players were at the dogs, Ladbrokes released their betting odds for the final. They made fascinating reading ...

> *Arsenal were 8-11 to win, West Ham 4-1*
> *The draw was 4-1.*
>
> *Arsenal to win 1-0 ... 7-1*
> *West Ham to win 1-0 ... 11-1*
> *Arsenl to win 2-0 ... 8-1*
> *West Ham to win 2-0 ... 20-1*
> *A goalless or 1-1 draw ... 7-1*
>
> *Odds on first player to score:*
> *Frank Stapleton and Alan Sunderland ... both 7-1*
> *David Cross for West Ham ... 9-1*
> *Trevor Brooking first player to score ... 25-1*

The odds quickly started shortening when an army of West Ham fans dived in at the juicy 4-1 price. There was also a lot of money laid on Ray Stewart to be the first goalscorer at the inviting odds of 14-1. And there was a fair amount of support for Trevor Brooking to be first on the scoresheet. If it had been for a headed goal, the punters would have wanted odds of at least 100-1!

Another popular bet was the draw at 7-1, inspired by the fact that Arsenal had become the Cup replay kings. It would be the first replay since Chelsea beat Leeds 2-1 after a 2-2 draw at Wembley in the 1970 final.

BBC and ITV cleared their daily schedules for wall-to-wall coverage of the final, and while the West Ham players were relaxing in their hotels watching the pre-match build-up they found themselves being given extra incentive to go out and win the match against all the odds.

Alan Mullery, Fulham's skipper when West Ham had beaten them in the 1975 FA Cup final, told viewers: "Hammers are going to get hammered. Their central defenders Bonds and Martin are not in the same class as Young and O'Leary in the middle of the Arsenal defence."

Bonzo and Martin had been nicely wound up!

Then Brian 'Motormouth' Clough repeated to ITV viewers what he had told the *Daily Express*: "They rave about that Trevor Brooking, and – to quote the great man Muhmmad Ali – he certainly does float like a butterfly ... and stings like one, too ..."

Trevor heard it, smiled to himself and felt an extra urge to help the Hammers win the Cup.

In that FA Cup final week, Trevor did a series of interviews with his good friend Peter Watson, a Fleet Street maestro who had been Sports Editor of the London *Evening News* and was about to take charge at the *Sunday Express*.

Trevor gave a fascinating professional view of the match on the morning of the final:

'Arsenal have perfected the art of getting men behind the ball, closing the space down and breaking from deep into dangerous situations.

That was never better illustrated than in the last two Cup semi-final replays with Liverpool. They scored in the opening moments of the second replay and it took mighty Liverpool virutally the whole 90 minutes to score the one goal that kept them alive.

Then Arsenal scored early on through Brian Talbot in the third replay, and Liverpool – with all their attacking strengths – could not break through the Arsenal barrier.

It gives you some idea of the task facing us at Wembley today. We've had a couple of team talks this week trying to pinpoint the strengths and weaknesses of the Arsenal side. And, as so many sides have found out during their three years of astonishing Cup runs, they have few weaknesses.

I am a great admirer of their front two – Frank Stapleton and Alan Sunderland. It is not just their attacking play, but it's what they do when they lose the ball that impresses the pros in the game.

They work so hard at closing down defenders when they lose possession that it gives Arsenal's game an extra dimension.

Stapleton is particularly strong in the air, and a master at knocking the ball down to Sunderland or one of the midfield players roaring through in support.

Sunderland gives Arsenal width on the right, which means they can have variations in the direction of their attack. This takes the pressure off their gifted left-sided players Liam Brady and Graham Rix.

Liam is supremely talented and is is one of the most creative players in Europe. That left-foot of his is deadly and he glides past opponents as if they were not there.

Some people feel he plays too deep. That is not my view. He deliberately lurks deep in the Arsenal half and comes forward when the time is right and there is space to exploit. We'll be watching for those long, raking passes of his that can open up any defence.

We shall also be keeping a close watch on Brian Talbot. He is the powerhouse of the Arsenal midfield, and the perfect partner for Liam and Graham.

Alan Sunderland, more bubbly than even the bubbling Hammers

He has played at Wembley so many times that the final is almost a home match for him. I've always said he gives the impression of having an extra lung. He just never stops running, and sacrifices his own considerable skills for the sake of the team. While his role is mainly defensive, he can come through undetected to pick up crucial goals.

Arsenal are famously rock solid at the back, with great goalkeeper Pat Jennings forming a holy trinity with central defenders Willie Young and David O'Leary.

Pat Rice is as good a right-back as there is in the First Division, and it will be interesting to see whether the very capable John Devine partners him or smooth-as-silk Sammy Nelson, a real footballing full-back.

So when you analyse the Arsenal team you wonder if there's any point in turning up! But hold on, we have all-round strength and skill, and in Alan Devonshire the most improved midfield player in the country.

Phil Parkes has been in Pat Jennings-type form this season. There can be no higher praise, and energetic young players like Paul Allen and Geoff Pike have come through and grown in stature and confidence with every game.

Crossy is as dangerous a striker as there is if given any space, and Stuart Pearson alongside him has been there, done that and knows the way to goal.

Billy Bonds and Alvin Martin are fantastic competitors and have developed a great partnership in the middle of the defence, and our full-backs Ray Stewart and Frank Lampard are both disciplined and determined.

We are expecting Arsenal to come at us at one helluva pace and we must be completely focused from the first whistle. People who have not seen us will I think be pleasantly surprised by the football that we play. It is much better than you would expect from a Second Division team.

I'm not a betting man, but if I were I would be hugely tempted by those 4-1 odds. Don't be at all surprised if you hear victory choruses of Bubbles filling Wembley at the final whistle.

Yes, Arsenal are the clear favourites, but we are quietly confident that we can cause an upset.'

John Lyall told the players just before they left the Wembley dressing-room for the challenge of their lifetimes: "You have done the club and yourselves proud by getting this far, but the job is only half done. Now go and finish it off by showing Arsenal that you are not only every bit as good as them ... you are better."

We now all waited to see what the big Lyall plan was as he led Hammers out into the hot house that was Wembley on this baking-hot Saturday May 10 1980. Let the game begin ...

THE 1980 FA CUP FINAL

WEMBLEY STADIUM,
May 10 1980

Attendance: 100,000

Referee: George Courtney
(Spennymoor, Co Durham)
Teams:

WEST HAM UNITED	ARSENAL
1 Phil Parkes	1 Pat Jennings
2 Ray Stewart	2 Pat Rice (captain)
3 Frank Lampard	3 John Devine
4 Billy Bonds (captain)	4 Brian Talbot
5 Alvin Martin	5 David O'Leary
6 Alan Devonshire	6 Willie Young
7 Paul Allen	7 Liam Brady
8 Stuart Pearson	8 Alan Sunderland
9 David Cross	9 Frank Stapleton
10 Trevor Brooking	10 David Price
11 Geoff Pike	11 Graham Rix
12 Paul Brush	12 Sammy Nelson

Managers:
John Lyall (West Ham), Terry Neill (Arsenal)

John Lyall and Billy Bonds cast shadows over Arsenal as they lead the Hammers out at Wembley

YOU could have fried an egg on the scorching hot Wembley pitch as managers John Lyall and Terry Neill led the teams out for a final being watched around the world by an audience of millions … and it was Arsenal who were about to be boiled.

The John Lyall plan was bold, yet simple. He went against all his principles about playing attacking football to come up with a formation designed to stop Arsenal from operating.

The Lyall Plot was to deny the Gunners the ball. "I was very aware that Arsenal had players with the skill to take us apart if we allowed them to," John revealed later in a series of interviews with his old friend Norman Giller. "But without the ball their creators were redundant. I instructed Paul Allen to sit on Liam Brady and Geoff Pike to do the same disciplined marking job on Graham Rix. It worked like a dream. Paul and Geoff were just unbelievable Nobody, not even seasoned professionals, could have done a better job."

Rather than their usual 4-4-2, Hammers lined up in a 4-5-1 shape: At the back, Stewart-Bonds-Martin-Lampard, and across the middle Allen-Brooking-Devonshire-Pike, with Stuart Pearson ordered to play deep just in front of them.

This put huge responsibility on the shoulders of David Cross as the lone striker on a day when the sun turned Wembley into a furnace. Crossy deserved a medal for gallantry let along his Cup winners' medal. He ran himself into the ground for the team.

For the Lyall plan to work to perfection it needed two things: 1) Players to run marathon distances at sprinter's speed; 2) a goal as early as possible to help heap the pressure on Arsenal.

In record-breaker Paul Allen and the determined, unselfish Geoff Pike, John had found the ideal grafters. They were prepared to run all day to make the lives of Liam Brady and Graham Rix a misery.

The vital goal came with the stopwatch showing 12 minutes 58 seconds, and from the most unlikely of sources – the educated head of Trevor Brooking.

It was Brooking's ever-improving apprentice Alan Devonshire who lay the foundations to the goal with a foraging left-wing run. Arsenal back-pedalled close to panic as he travelled first-class with pace and authority.

Suddenly he fired over a cross that swerved tantalisingly beyond the reach of master goalkeeper Pat Jennings. The ball fell into the path of David Cross, whose instant shot ricocheted off Arsenal legs and on to the radar screen of Stuart Pearson. He was standing virtually in the same spot where he scored for Manchester United against Liverpool in the 1977 FA Cup final. Pearson fired right-footed but failed to make a proper connection, and the ball screwed knee-high across the face of the Arsenal goal. The ball was there for whoever wanted it, almost giftwrapped. It was Trevor Brooking who was quickest to react, scoring in instalments as he went down on his knees and glance-headed the ball off his forehead and wide of a startled Pat Jennings, who was still regrouping after having set himself to save first from Cross and then Pearson. It all happened quicker than it took to write that last sentence, yet was a moment that became etched into the memory of all those who saw it.

Let's be honest, it was not the greatest goal ever witnessed at Wembley, probably not even in the top 100. But for those looking through claret and blue glasses it was an absolute cracker, and the fact that it came off Brooking's head took it into the realms of fantasy. In the press box, nobody could remember Trevor ever having headed a goal before, an amazing stat-fact that Trevor himself later confirmed.

"Are you watching Brian Clough?" came the taunting chants from the wildly celebrating West Ham supporters hot on the heels of the inevitable choruses of Bubbles. Arsenal's fans had been stunned into silence.

Cloughie had sneeringly said before the match that Brooking floated like a butterfly and stung like one. The goal must have been like a bee sting on the bum for Old Big 'Ead, as he worked as co-commentator alongside ITV's Brian Moore.

The game now became like a physical game of chess as Arsenal tried to get themselves out of a check-mate situation. But the moves they had been perfecting all season in their hunt for four major trophies were just not working against the disciplined and determined Hammers. They were like orchestra players who could not quite get their instruments in tune.

Everywhere an Arsenal player went a Hammer was sure to go. Liam Brady found himself wearing Paul Allen like a second skin, Graham Rix was shadowed by Geoff Pike and Billy Bonds was running through any Gunner who got in his way. Bonzo was giving an extraordinary exhibition of how to lead by example. Socks down around his ankles and bathed in perspiration, he was making it as hot as hell for the Arsenal forwards. Full-backs Stewart and Lampard were curbing their appetite for adventurous overlapping runs and picking up any Arsenal player seeking space, while Alvin Martin in the middle was as solid as if imported from the Himalayas rather than Merseyside.

Phil Parkes had so little to do that he was later able to say it was one of his easiest games of the season.

At the other end there was bewilderment. The Lyall tactics had got Arsenal completely flummoxed to the point where a baffled David O'Leary was overheard shouting to Terry Neill and Don Howe on the bench: "I've got nobody to mark …"

Artist Art Turner's impressionist view of Trevor Brooking's goal celebration with Billy Bonds

Alvin Martin and the capped Paul Allen on a celebration tour of Wembley

Willie Young had his hands full tracking the solo running of David Cross, while full-backs Pat Rice and John Devine were, like O'Leary, virtually redundant. The players they were expecting to be marking – Paul Allen, Alan Devonshire and Stuart Pearson – were way back in a midfield as packed as Green Street market on a Saturday.

Devonshire and Trevor Brooking saw a lot more of the ball than the Arsenal schemers and concentrated on keeping it rather than showing their usual adventure. Several of the Gunners defenders were in danger of getting sunburned tongues as they chased claret and blue shadows.

Arsenal gathered themselves for a big push in the second-half after half-time pep talks from Terry Neill and Don Howe but, while they had more possession, they gradually ran out of passion as they were continually pushed wide. They were unable to strike at the heart of the Hammers defence, and big Phil Parkes was troubled even less than in the first-half.

West Ham were giving a masterclass in how to defend without resorting to violence or an over-emphasis on muscularity. The Gunners began to look physically and mentally tired, their hard slog of a season taking its toll. They sent on full-back Sammy Nelson as substitute for John Devine in the 62nd minute, but they needed a forward with fresh legs to take on the Hammers defence. Sammy was never going to be up to that sort of challenge.

When, a few weeks earlier, Hammers had lost out on their first priority of promotion back to the First Division there were blind (barmy even) West Ham fans who called for John Lyall's head. Now they were chorusing his name as it became clear he had tactically out-thought Arsenal while his players outfought them.

It was a magnificent team performance, with West Ham's Musketeer all-for-one-and-one-for-all spirit shining through. For Paul Allen in particular, it was an unforgettable experience. He had been one of the coolest players in the dressing-room beforehand and was totally focused on the assignment given to him by John Lyall. Paul followed the advice of his professional footballer Dad to 'play your natural game.'

There could and should have been a glorious climax to Paul's record-breaking day. He broke through on a solo run in the closing moments of the match, outpaced Graham Rix and was on his way to a one-on-one duel with the great Pat Jennings when Willie Young cynically chopped him down from behind.

Every West Ham fan and all the neutrals were enraged by the ruthless professional foul, and even some Arsenal supporters jeered a moment that robbed the then youngest ever finalist at Wembley of the opportunity for a fairytale end to his adventure. In the modern game Young would have got an instant red card. He got away with a yellow.

It was a sad end to an intense match that Arsenal wanted to forget as quickly as possible, while – thirty years on – everybody with claret and blue blood remembers it as one of the great games in Hammers history … surely worth a book!

CAPTAIN Fantastic Billy Bonds led the West Ham players on a deliriously happy parade of the pitch after collecting the FA Cup from the Duchess of Kent. Newish Prime Minister Margaret Thatcher was in the Royal Box and said: "Well done, Mr Bonds."

It had been a prime performance by Billy and the boys, and they lined-up to tell their stories as they became engulfed by press, television and radio reporters in the madhouse that was the West Ham dressing-room and later at the after-match banquet. Let's listen in:

JOHN LYALL: "My plan worked to perfection, but all the credit must go to the players not me. I asked each of them to do a specific job and not one of them failed. If it had gone wrong, I would have held my hands up and taken the blame, but thanks to the efforts of the players out there on the pitch it went right.

It meant in several cases they had to sacrifice the chance of individual glory, but that is never a problem at West Ham. We believe in the team ethic. I got the idea for our change of tactics after watching the second semi-final replay between Arsenal and Liverpool, but it was not until as late as Thursday that we tried it out in training.

I lost sleep wondering if perhaps I should take the easy way out and simply switch Ray Stewart to do a man-marking job in midfield on Liam Brady. But I knew we needed that extra man in midfield to negate the skill of Brady and Rix and the power running of Talbot and Price. This meant putting a lot on the shoulders of Stuart Pearson and David Cross. I got Stuart to play deeper than he'd ever played before, and asked David to take the responsibility of being a lone striker, with support coming through if and when we had possession. He accepted the job without a murmur of complaint.

As I led the team out, the strong spring sunshine made me wonder if I had asked too much. David was going to have to do a lot of running in unexpectedly hot conditions, but he just got on with it and played a massive part in our victory.

Paul Allen was just remarkable. Instead of being attacked by Wembley nerves, he was the one who was settling everybody else down. He is seventeen going on twenty-seven. He and Geoff Pike were key parts of my plan. I told

Paul to make his main priority stopping the ball reaching Liam Brady and, when he was in possession, to give him as little time and space as possible. I rate Liam one of Europe's finest creative players, but Paul didn't give him time or space in which to breathe. Geoff had a similar brief with Graham Rix and just stifled the life out of him. I doubt if Brady and Rix have ever been so ineffective, and it was all down to the energy and discipline of our two home-grown lads. I am so proud of them.

I was off my bench thinking Paul was going to score in the last moments, until Willie Young brought him down. It was an appalling tackle, and Willie will have to live with what he did. You could tell by the crowd reaction that few people condoned those sort of tactics in what was mainly a sporting contest in the true spirit of the game. What pleased me is the way Paul did not make a meal of it. He got up and even shook Willie's hand. That's the sort of sportsmanship we breed and encourage at West Ham.

Billy Bonds was, of course, immense. I have never ever known him give less than 100 per cent at all times. I doubt if we would have the Cup if the disciplinary committeee had suspended him, which at one time seemed likely. He and Alvin Martin did not allow Stapleton and Sunderland a sniff of goal all afternoon, and Ray Stewart and Frank Lampard were always there in support if necessary. Phil Parkes cannot believe he had so little to do.

As for our twin schemers, I thought Brooking and Devonshire looked a class above any of the Arsenal players. They were so composed on the ball. It is almost unbelievable what Alan has achieved in such a short space of time. It seems like only yesterday that he was playing with Southall, and here he is firmly established as one of the finest midfield players in the country.

Trevor never ceases to amaze me with his skill and authority, but today he astonished even himself by scoring with his head. If somebody had predicted before the game that we would win 1-0 with a headed goal by Trevor Brooking I would have wondered what sort of drug they were on.

We now have to quickly pull ourselves together ready for Monday's League trip to Sunderland. Our old mate Geoff Hurst at Chelsea will not forgive us if we don't do our best to win there.*

Note: Hammers lost 2-0 and Geoff Hurst's Chelsea failed to get promotion.

TERRY NEILL: ❝Sincere congratulations to West Ham. They deserved their victory. It would be easy to blame our defeat on the exhausting semi-final marathon, but that is an excuse we will not be making. On the day, West Ham were the better team and they managed to stop us from playing our usual game. I have to say it was not the sort of performance we expected from a West Ham team who usually like to come out to play. Today they were content to sit back and fill the midfield with bodies so that the game never ebbed and flowed. It became a stalemate in midfield. I have already said my piece to our players about going to sleep for their goal. That ball should have been cleared long before Brooking got his head to it. Our job now is to pick ourselves up and focus on the European Cup Winners' Cup final in Brussels on Wednesday ...❞

Note: Arsenal lost on a penalty shoot-out to Valencia and they finished their season empty-handed.

BILLY BONDS: ❝I shared a room at our hotel last night with Alvin Martin and we read an article in *The Sun* by Malcolm Macdonald in which he said we'd struggle against Frank Stapleton and Alan Sunderland, me because of my age and Alvin because of his lack of pace. Then on television Alan Mullery said we would get roasted. It was just what we needed to motivate us. They are entitled to their opinions but when you see fellow pros putting the boot in it gives you that extra edge to your game. So thank you Malcolm and Mullers!❞

PHIL PARKES: ❝I could have taken a deckchair out and enjoyed the sunshine! Bonzo and Alvin were magnificent, and I had one of my easiest games of the season. We closed Arsenal down so well they just could not get in any shots. All I had to deal with was a hopeful curling shot from Graham Rix in the first-half that I pushed around the post, and in the second-half there was a long-range free-kick by Brian Talbot that I caught comfortably. I cut out a few crosses and that was about it. We did not give Arsenal a look in. We all made a fuss of Paul Allen. What memories he's got. He's hardly started shaving and now he has an FA Cup winners' medal. Before the game he was walking around the dressing-room smiling as if he was getting ready to play in a local parks match. What a career he's got ahead of him.❞

Billy Bonds delivers the FA Cup to the West Ham fans at Wembley

PAUL ALLEN: 'Everybody is asking me what I thought about Willie Young's tackle. I don't want to make anything of it. What he did he did for his team, and he may have saved me embarrassing myself by making a mess of the chance. What I do know is that as I got nearer and nearer to the goal Pat Jennings seemed to be growing in size. He was not going to make it easy for me to score, that's for sure. I cried a little at the end, but they were tears of sheer joy. I looked up and found my family in the ground and that's when the tears came. Mum and Dad had supported me all the way and they were part of my magical day. Everything had gone perfectly. Now I'm off to join the England youth team and will miss the League match at Sunderland. It's been quite a season!'

DAVID CROSS: 'It was a masterstroke of tactics by John Lyall. When he told Stuart Pearson and I what he wanted us to do I thought to myself that it was quite a gamble, and for twenty minutes I was still wondering if it was right. Then I saw David O'Leary looking completely baffled and shouting to the touchline bench, "I've got nobody to mark ..." That's when I knew we had them. They just did not know how to counter John's tactics. It has been a frustrating season for me with injuries, but this has made it all worthwhile. To win the FA Cup when we are a Second Division side is a bit special, and we will now have the confidence to go on and get the First Division place that we feel entitled to.'

ALAN DEVONSHIRE: 'Bonzo had said to soak up the atmosphere because it would all be over so quickly. He had been there five years earlier when he led Hammers to their victory over Fulham. So when I went out on the pitch beforehand I tried to capture it all for my memory. The Arsenal players were out on the pitch at the same time, and I thought they looked tense and anxious compared with us. I was glad to play a part in the goal. There was not a lot of space all afternoon, but I found some down the left-wing and managed to get past Graham Rix and Pat Rice before crossing the ball towards the far post. The next few seconds were a blur of action before Trevor went down on his knees to head the ball into the net. What a moment that was for the entire team. I'll never forget it, and neither will Trevor!'

THE world and his brother wanted to interview Trevor Brooking at the end of his remarkable match. It was *Express* Newspapers executive Peter Watson, Trevor's close friend, who came up with these startling Monday morning exclusive comments from the Hammers goalscoring hero:

TREVOR BROOKING: •I hope that Brian Clough has learned his lesson and won't in future launch scathing attacks like the one he made on me on the morning of the final. His timing was unbelievable.

It was not only his cheap crack about me stinging like a butterfly but his statement that he has never ever rated me that caused me to raise my eyebrows.

This from the mouth of the man who tried to sign me – and my then clubmate Bobby Moore – when he was managing at Derby County.

I'm experienced enough and old enough not to worry about Clough's comments and let them get under my skin. But if he had said it about a younger player I wonder how he would have reacted.

It was the main topic of conversation on the morning of the match, and I knew the only way I wanted to reply was on the pitch.

I feel I gave the perfect response. To score the only goal of the match wasn't bad for a butterfly.

I often wonder if Clough is controversial for the sake of it. Only he knows the answer to that. But he attacks his own players publicly, too. Perhaps he thinks that is the way to motivate them. I find it strange.

I certainly didn't need motivating for Saturday's final. John Lyall's style is in complete contrast to that of Clough. He likes to have a quiet word individually with each player, telling them what he wants from them.

What a masterstroke he played on Saturday in playing Stuart Pearson in midfield. It completely confused Arsenal.

John didn't reveal his full plan until Saturday. It was foreign to most of us to have to play with an eye more on defence than attack, but the result proved that John knew what he was doing.

I am still in shock after scoring with my head! I said to big Pat Jennings as we came out for the second-half, 'That's the first goal I've ever scored with

my head, Pat. It's a minor miracle.' One of the nicest blokes in the game, Pat chuckled and said: 'I didn't even know it was you who scored. I was too busy getting the ball out of the net. I'll never live it down. Getting beaten by a Brooking header ...'

I had got myself into the Arsenal six-yard box to try to get on the end of Alan Devonshire's cross. It fell to David Cross, whose shot was smothered. Then Stuart Pearson had a go and the ball squirted across the face of goal.

The ball was going behind me and I dipped back and went down to meet it with my head. It was going so fast that I knew I only had to connect and it would be in the net.

As I celebrated I thought of my little daughter Collette. When I left home on Friday to join the team she said: "Score a goal for me, Daddy."

"I'll do my best darling," I told her, not thinking for one second that it would be with my head! Now that was a goal with a real sting.'

There was a strange sequel to the Clough/Brooking story seven years later after Trevor had retired. He was working as a co-commentator for BBC radio in a Cup tie between Crystal Palace and Cloughie's Nottingham Forest at Selhurst Park.

Standing alone in the tunnel before the match, he was aware of the Forest dressing-room door opening. Suddenly, almost furtively, Cloughie came out and stood beside him.

"Young man," Cloughie said, "before the FA Cup final in 1980 I made some comments about you that were right out of order. I'm extremely sorry and I wish to apologise."

He shook Trevor's hand, and then disappeared back into the dressing-room as quickly and as quietly as he had appeared.

Trevor said: "I was amazed. All those years later and he still felt he owed me an apology. That was a big thing to do, and I respected him for it."

The day after the final the West Ham players paraded with the Cup in an open coach through the streets of East London. Police estimated that the turn out was more than 250,000 people.

"We got an unbelievable greeting" said skipper Billy Bonds. "It was one of the most emotional afternoons of my life. I don't think I've ever seen so many grown men crying." Hammers were really bubbling.

FOR those of us who were around at the time, it seems inconceivable that thirty years have gone by since West Ham won the FA Cup on that unforgettable Saturday May 10 1980. It seems like only the day before yesterday that Billy Bonds was cavorting around Wembley with his socks down around his ankles and the FA Cup trophy raised above his head. We have tried hard to trace what happened to each of the Hammers' heroes after that memorable victory over Arsenal. We kick-off with the mastermind of the triumph, who sadly is no longer with us ...

JOHN LYALL: The most successful manager in West Ham's history, John was controversially sacked in 1989 after 34 years service to the club. It was shameful the way the Board treated him in the last weeks of his career at Upton Park, but it could not take away the legacy he had left behind. He dedicated himself to carrying on the standards of fair play, sportsmanship and skill that had been instigated by his mentor Ron Greenwood.

The then Tottenham manager Terry Venables employed John as a scout until Ipswich appointed him their manager in May 1990. Two years later he guided Ipswich to promotion as Second Division champions before retiring in 1994 to concentrate on his love of gardening. It was a huge shock when he died suddenly of a heart attack in 2006 at the age of 66, just two weeks after attending the funeral of Ron Greenwood, who also passed away in Suffolk at the age of 84.

The then Hammers manager Alan Pardew acted as spokesman for the club: "On behalf of all our staff and players, I first of all wish to pass on my sincere condolences to John's wife, Yvonne, his son Murray, his grandchildren and the rest of his family. It is another very sad day for West Ham United after the loss of Ron Greenwood just two months ago and, like Ron, John did so much to build the footballing beliefs and values that this club is built on.

"To win the FA Cup twice and lead the club to its highest-ever League finish tells you just how much of an impact John Lyall made on the history of West Ham United, and his contribution will never be forgotten. I am sure that our supporters will pay tribute to John's memory in a fitting manner at our FA Cup semi-final at Villa Park on Sunday and we as a team will do the same."

Trevor Brooking said: "It's a huge shock. He was a much-loved figure at Upton Park and had a lasting influence on the club's development and the way

the team played. Like Ron Greenwood before him, he encouraged good, open attacking football and all West Ham fans will be deeply shocked by today's news. He was a man of great integrity and loyalty and anyone who knew him would have nothing but good things to say about him.

"He recently attended a players' reunion and was easily the most popular man that evening. Everyone wanted to talk to him. I think everyone in football will feel a sense of loss today and our thoughts at the moment are with his wife and family."

Billy Bonds, John's skipper during the good times, said: "He was a brilliant coach, a totally honest man and you could trust everything he said. After finishing playing because of injury, he turned himself into one of the greatest coaches of any era. He was the most successful manager of the club but above all he was a very honest man and a family man. You wouldn't hear a bad word said about him by anyone in football."

John was admired and liked throughout the game. Former Ipswich manager Sir Bobby Robson said: "He was a proper person and a proper football coach. He was respected by players and loved the game, wanting it to be played in the right spirit. He was a disciplinarian, but that was more through his attitude towards the game than wanting to prove himself the boss. John was very democratic and would listen as well as give the best possible instructions. He is a big loss to the game and to the human race."

There was a mass turn out of former players when a blue plaque was erected at the Boleyn Ground in January 2008 in John's memory and, in December 2009, West Ham renamed the main entrance at Upton Park The John Lyall Gates.

PHIL PARKES: After playing 344 League games for the Hammers, Phil followed John Lyall to Ipswich in 1990 and played just three Second Division games for the Suffolk club He then concentrated on a backroom coaching role, specialising in passing on his goalkeeping knowledge. He later coached at his old club Queens Park Rangers before going back into his original profession of carpentry. He started a successful building firm in Reading. In 2003, he was elected the goalkeeper in West Ham's all-time dream team – beating players of the calibre of Ernie Gregory and Ludek 'Ludo' Miklosko.

Thirty years on, Frank Lampard Snr co-owner of a trendy Chelsea pub with Frank Lampard Jnr

RAY STEWART: After building legendary status in the game with his extraordinary record from the penalty spot, Ray returned home to Scotland in 1991. He played briefly for St Johnstone and Stirling Albion until having to give in to old injury problems. Ray coached and then tried with little luck to establish himself as a manager, with Stirling, Livingston and Forfar Athletic. He failed to make an impact with any of the clubs, and made the local headlines in 2004 when he took a job as a chauffeur. One thing's for sure, he was never ever a passenger when playing for West Ham as a defender with dynamite in his right foot.

FRANK LAMPARD: He has always been the perfect partner, first as a dependable and often inspiring West Ham full-back and then assistant manager/coach to his brother-in-law Harry Redknapp at Upton Park (1994-2001). While Frank Junior was getting all the headlines, Frank Senior was teaming up with Brendan Rodgers – Jose Mourinho's former coach at Stamford Bridge – in a consultancy role at Watford and Reading. Since leaving West Ham in 2001 Frank Senior's main focus has been on property development, including co-owning a trendy pub off the King's Road with Frank Junior, who left the Hammers for Chelsea under a cloud of controversy in 2001 after his Dad and 'Uncle' Harry had been sacked.

BILLY BONDS: Following his club record 793 first-team appearances for West Ham, Bonzo had four years as manager of the Hammers before leaving in acrimonious circumstances when his assistant Harry Redknapp succeeded him in 1994. He has since been in charge of the Queens Park Rangers youth squad and had a short, unsuccessful spell as manager of Millwall. These day Billy spends a lot of time in the Spanish sunshine, and on his return visits to Upton Park – a ground where he once vowed never to set foot again – he gets the hero's welcome he deserves. The Hammers have rarely had a more loyal and productive player, who must have trodden on every blade of grass at Upton Park in his 21 years of dedicated service. How sad that it all ended in tears, with Billy accusing the board of working behind his back. In numerous Polls, he invariably comes third in the vote for the all-time great Hammers behind Bobby Moore and Trevor Brooking.

ALVIN MARTIN: One of West Ham's finest ever centre-halves, Alvin played 600 games during his 19 years at Upton Park before ending his playing days 'down the road' at the Orient. He was badly bruised by his two seasons of experience as a manager at struggling Southend United from 1997 until 1999. A Scouser with a sharp sense of humour and usually with something sensible to say, Alvin switched to the microphone and became an excellent commentator and pundit for TalkSport. He has not done badly for a kid who had his heart broken when Everton rejected him as a teenager. Everton's loss was West Ham's gain.

ALAN DEVONSHIRE: He collected eight England caps after his success in the 1979-80 season and stayed at the Hammers for another ten years before moving on in 1990 for a couple of seasons with Watford. Alan started a non-League management career with Maidenhead and then took charge of Blue Square South side Hampton & Richmond in 2003. He is widely acknowledged as one of the most accomplished and best organised managers outside the Football League and it is a mystery as to why one of the established clubs have not poached him. Alan always talks warmly of his days with the Hammers, and particularly of the good influence John Lyall had on him both as a footballer and as a man.

PAUL ALLEN: His great football playing adventure that started with a bang at Wembley ended with a whimper down in Purfleet where he had his last kicks in 1998. In between Paul played 370 games for Tottenham, where his Uncle Les and cousin Clive were goalscoring legends. After Spurs – with whom he played in the FA Cup finals of 1987 and 1991 – Paul travelled the football roundabout with Southampton, Luton Town, Stoke City, Bristol City and Millwall. He never forgot the grounding he received at the acclaimed West Ham youth academy, and has passed on valuable knowledge to a conveyor belt of other coaches in his role as Professional Footballers' Association 'super' coach, with the South-East as his main patch. While remembered with great affection by West Ham supporters who were around in 1980, Paul now regards himself more as a White Hart Lane man, and has been inducted into the Tottenham Hall of Fame, following Uncle Les and cousin Clive.

Thirty years on, Paul Allen coaches the coaches for the Professional Footballers' Association

STUART PEARSON: Despite the knee injury that forced him to give up his short but eventful Hammers career in 1982, 'Pancho' Pearson still managed to get in a couple of seasons playing down in South Africa and then, briefly, in the North American Soccer League. He then returned to the UK in 1985 to coach at Stockport County and manage Northwich Victoria before becoming assistant boss to Brian Talbot at West Bromwich. He left Albion in 1992 and was assistant manager at Bradford City from 1992 to 1994. He appears regularly on MUTV on his trips back from Spain, where he spends most of his retirement time.

DAVID CROSS: After his 77 goals in 179 League games for the Hammers, David became a footballing nomad. From 1982 he played for Manchester City, Vancouver Whitecaps, Oldham Athletic, West Bromwich Albion, Bolton Wanderers and Bury before taking his final shots in Cyprus with AEL Limassol. He dabbled in the world of insurance before returning to the game as coach and then assistant manager at Oldham. His son, Robert, and daughters Jennifer and Kathryn have all had active sporting careers, each of them playing cricket to a high standard. Jennifer has also featured in the national netball super league. David was welcomed back at Upton Park in the capacity of chief scout.

TREVOR BROOKING: Of all the ex-Hammers, none have had quite as astonishing a success story since leaving the club as Trevor – Sir Trevor – Brooking. His long-playing record with West Ham ended in 1984 after 88 goals in 528 League games plus THAT headed goal in the 1980 FA Cup final. He lifted his England caps collection to 47, finishing in the final match of his mentor Ron Greenwood's 1982 World Cup campaign. He made two guest appearances for Cork City and then settled down to a busy and productive life in and out of football. His output has included chairman of Sport England, Director of Football Development with the FA, expert summariser on BBCtv and BBC radio, two caretaker spells as emergency manager at Upton Park, and running his book binding and printing business that he started early in his career as a player. He has been rewarded with the MBE, the CBE and then a knighthood in 2004, and he has a stand named in his honour at Upton Park.

Thirty years on, Hammers heroes Billy Bonds, Ray Stewart, Alan Devonshire and Phil Parkes

GEOFF PIKE: In all, Geoff scored 42 goals in 373 appearances for the Hammers before moving on to Notts County in 1987. He netted 17 goals in 82 League matches for Notts and then moved back to East London to hold his passing out parade with Leyton Orient. Geoff scored one goal in 44 League games before hanging up his boots in 1991. Like Paul Allen, he became a 'super' coach with the Professional Footballers' Association. He coached the coaches at fourteen clubs in the South East, at youth and senior level. After nine years in this role, he was promoted to 'head office' at the Football Association – working closely with old clubmate Sir Trevor Brooking – as they concentrated on improving English football at grassroots level.

PAUL BRUSH: He played a crucial part in West Ham's run to the FA Cup final, and was accepted as very much a part of the squad in the Final, though wearing the No 12 substitute's shirt. After his 151 League appearances for the Hammers, Paul played for Crystal Palace, Southend United, Enfield and Heybridge Swifts before having a crack at management with Leyton Orient, where he had been an enthusiastic coach. He was sacked by the Os after two seasons of struggle, and then became assistant manager to Steve Tilson at Southend. They steered the club to two successive promotions from League Two to the Championship, but Paul was dismissed in March 2010 after more than six years at Roots Hall.

WEST HAM's past is inexorably and gloriously wrapped up with Wembley. It took the Hammers to open the Stadium – along with Bolton Wanderers – with one of the most famous matches in football history. This is our version of the story, the first of four Wembley tales that preceded the 1980 FA Cup final ...

The Football Association had a contract with a new stadium that was being built in Middlesex for the 1924 British Empire Exhibition. It was called, simply, The Empire Stadium, but was soon to be known to everybody in football as Wembley. It would become synonymous with all that was best and, just occasionally, the worst about the English game.

It was football that had the honour of being the first event at the magnificent, twin-towered stadium. On 28 April 1923, Bolton Wanderers played West Ham United in what has gone down in football folklore as the White Horse final.

As the new stadium had been built to hold 127,000 spectators, the Football Association and the ground owners did not even consider making the match all-ticket. Right up until the day of the final, newspaper advertisements and posters were urging football fans to get to Wembley to see history being made ... the first match at the Empire Stadium.

It had been erected at a cost of £750,000 in just three hundred working days. Workmen, including German prisoners of war, used 25,000 tons of concrete, 1,500 tons of steel and half a million rivets (contrast that with the Millennium Dome which took three years to build at a cost of £750-million and rising).

The final work was carried out just three days before the FA Cup final. By the time the game was over, there was a lot more work needed doing – repairing gates that had been smashed down by the milling mob that got in without paying.

The FA had spectacularly underestimated the interest in the first match at the new stadium. It was calculated that more than 200,000 people got in to see the game, a little matter of 73,000 over the ground's capacity. The wonder is that nobody was killed as thousands of fans spilled on the pitch to the point where not a blade of grass could be seen. Wembley's new turf, the first sod of which was laid by the future King George VI, was in danger of drowning under a human tide.

THE 1923 FA CUP FINAL

WEMBLEY STADIUM,
April 28 1923

Bolton Wanderers 2, West Ham United 0
Scorers: David Jack, Jack Smith (Bolton)
Attendance: 126,047
Referee: D. H. Asson
(West Bromwich)

BOLTON WANDERERS

1 Dick Pym
2 Bob Haworth
3 Alex FInney
4 Harry Nuttall
5 Jimmy Seddon
6 Billy Jennings
7 Billy Butler
8 David Jack
9 Jack Smith
10 Joe Smith (captain)
11 Ted Vizard

WEST HAM UNITED

1 Ted Hufton
2 Billy Henderson
3 Jack Young
4 Syd Bishop
5 George Kay (captain)
6 Jack Tresadern
7 Dick Richards
8 Billy Brown
9 Vic Watson
10 Billy Moore
11 Jimmy Ruffell

Managers:
Charles Foweraker (Bolton), Syd King (West Ham)

West Ham's goalscoring legend Vic Watson, a runner-up at Wembley in 1923

Slowly and patiently, a policeman on a white horse – the policeman Pc George Scorey, the horse Billy – nudged and nursed the spectators back to the touchlines. While all this was going on, desperately concerned officials discussed calling off the match. But it was pointed out that 1) this could enrage the crowd and cause more of a problem; 2) King George V was on his way by motorcar from Buckingham Palace as the VIP guest.

As the King arrived, the crowd broke spontaneously into the National Anthem and, miraculously, the game kicked off just forty-five minutes late.

West Ham, whose strength lay on the wings, were enormously handicapped by the fact that the crowd were on and often pitch-side of the touchline. Police had to drive an avenue through the tightly jammed fans every time a player took a corner, and there were many instances when the ball bounced back into play off spectators without a throw-in being awarded.

When Bolton inside-forward David Jack scored the first ever goal at Wembley in just two minutes, West Ham left-half Jack Tresadern was battling to try to get back on to the pitch after going into the packed crowd to retrieve the ball.

The players stayed on the pitch at half-time because they feared they might never get back on if they tried to battle their way to the dressing-rooms. Tresadern, who had made his England debut two weeks earlier, said:

"We could not see the players' tunnel. If we had gone off we might never have found the pitch again! The best pass I had all afternoon was from a spectator!"

Bolton's victory-clinching goal eight minutes into the second-half came from a rifled shot from Scotsman Jack Smith. It hit the human wall of spectators crammed against the back of the net and rebounded into play, with many people thinking it had hit a post.

West Ham trainer – later manager – Charlie Paynter attributed the West Ham defeat to the damage the pitch had suffered before kick-off. "It was that white horse thumping its big feet into the pitch that made it hopeless. Our wingers were tumbling all over the place, tripping up in great ruts and holes," he said.

The official attendance was given as 126,047, with 90,520 people paying at the turnstiles on the day and another 32,527 buying tickets in advance. The total income was £27,776 of which £4,206 went to the taxman, the stadium got £4,714, and the

FA and both teams received £6,365 1s 8d each. The final count would indicate that more than 70,000 fans got in without paying. Not all of the ticket holders managed to see the game, and £2,797 was refunded to people who could not either find their seat or get into the ground.

Not surprisingly, from then on all FA Cup finals were ticket-only affairs.

The season ended happily for West Ham. Two days later they won a vital Second Division promotion match at Sheffield Wednesday, and they went up to the First Division for the first time despite a final match defeat by Notts County.

We should not leave the historic first FA Cup final at Wembley without quoting the real hero of the afternoon, Pc George Scorey. He was interviewed by just about every newspaper in the land, and his 13-year-old horse, Billy, became even more famous than any ridden by popular champion jockey of the time, Steve Donoghue. This was George's story:

"I had my wedding coming up and that was the only thing on my mind at the time. When I was told to report for duty at Wembley I didn't think a lot of it because I'm not a keen follower of football. I could not believe it when I saw how many people came spilling on to the pitch. You could not see any of the ground, and there seemed no way the game could be played.

"All the credit must go to Billy. I almost reluctantly started to push people back over the touchline, convinced it was a hopeless task. He quickly got the idea and gently but firmly nosed them back. They were a good-natured lot, and moved back out of Billy's way without protest. I kept shouting, 'Clear the pitch, gentlemen … make room for the players. If you want to see the game, move back, please.'

"It took about forty minutes, I suppose. There were other policemen working hard, too, so don't give me all the praise. I stayed and watched the game, but was not that interested. I just wanted to get Billy home and fed. When my fiancée asked me what sort of day I'd had I replied, 'Nothing out of the ordinary, lass.' It was only when I saw the newspapers with dozens of photographs of Billy clearing the pitch that I realised we must have done something pretty special."

Charlie Paynter, West Ham trainer in 1923 and their manager from 1932 until 1950

IT was forty-one years before the Hammers were back at Wembley for an FA Cup final, and again it was against a Lancashire team – Preston North End. One of the most famous clubs in the land but now down in the Second Division. This is our account of the match ...

West Ham United's contribution to football in the Sixties stretched far beyond the boundaries of the domestic scene. They won the FA Cup and the European Cup Winners' Cup with stylish soccer that was tactically a decade ahead of its time. The three main motivators – Bobby Moore, Geoff Hurst and Martin Peters – would knit West Ham-designed moves into the England playing pattern and would be influential in the 1966 World Cup victory.

There have been more successful and resilient sides but rarely one as attractive and entertaining.

In the 1964 FA Cup final at Wembley they were given a thorough examination of their class and staying power by a Second Division Preston team that played football right out of the top drawer. Neutral fans would have felt great sympathy for Preston, who were level or in front for all but the last 90 seconds of the match. West Ham's skin-of-their-teeth victory provided the foundation for greater triumphs that lay ahead.

There were sneers that West Ham manager Ron Greenwood inherited so much young talent when he took over at Upton Park in 1961 that he could not have failed to capture major honours. But Greenwood, a master of soccer strategy, had the vision and the perception to mould and shape the team into a winning unit.

He spotted the true potential of Geoff Hurst, for instance, and converted him from an ordinary wing-half into a world-class striker.

Ron was a man of high principle who stood for all that was good and proper about football, and even when West Ham started to slide as other less talented teams concentrated on kicking their way to success, he continued to preach that the game should be played with style, panache and sportsmanship.

Bobby Moore was the kingpin of the West Ham defence, which was sometimes suspect under pressure. Bobby was considered by many to be the greatest defender who ever pulled on an England shirt, and he he was a super reader of sitatuations alongside the strong and reliable Ken Brown at centre-half. Jim Standen was an

THE 1964 FA CUP FINAL

WEMBLEY STADIUM,
May 2 1964

West Ham United 3, Preston North End 2
Half-time 1-2
Scorers: John Sissons, Geoff Hurst, Ronnie Boyce (West Ham)
Doug Holden, Alex Dawson (Preston)
Attendance: 100,000
Referee: Arthur Holland (Barnsley)

WEST HAM UNITED	PRESTON NORTH END
1 Jim Standen	1 Alan Kelly
2 John Bond	2 George Ross
3 Jack Burkett	3 Jim Smith
4 Eddie Bovington	4 Nobby Lawton (captain)
5 Ken Brown	5 Tony Singleton
6 Bobby Moore (captain)	6 Howard Kendall
7 Peter Brabrook	7 Davie Wilson
8 Ronnie Boyce	8 Alec Ashworth
9 Johnny Byrne	9 Alex Dawson
10 Geoff Hurst	10 Alan Spavin
11 John Sissons	11 Doug Holden

Managers:
Ron Greenwood (West Ham), Jimmy Milne (Preston)

John Sissons, the youngest goalscorer in a Wembley FA Cup final

agile and confident goalkeeper, and at full-back the flamboyant John Bond –"Muffin' because he could kick the ball like a mule – was partnered by the stylish Jack Burkett.

Ronnie Boyce was the heart of the Hammers in the midfield engine room. He was nicknamed 'Ticker' because his non-stop running and precise passing made the team tick. An unobtrusive player, he was always to be found where the action was – rarely taking the eye of the spectators, but his team-mates always knew exactly where to find him. Eddie Bovington played the role of anchorman, winning the ball and then distributing with sensible rather than spectacular passes. He was keeping a promising youngster called Martin Peters on the sidelines.

Johnny 'Budgie' Byrne, creative and with a nose for goals, was the perfect partner for the more positive Hurst in the middle of the West Ham attack – with Peter Brabrook and John Sissons providing width as orthodox wingers who could delivere pin-pointed centres. Sissons was just eighteen, and would have been the youngest ever Wembley finalist but for the fact that his England youth team-mate Howad Kendall was playing for Preston, and was still only seventeen.

'Kid' Kendall was at left-half in a Preston team that had a balanced mixture of youth and experience. Their forward line of Davie Wilson, Alec Ashworth, Alex Dawson, Alan Spavin and Doug Holden had been impressive all season. They had narrowly missed promotion to the First Division after being pipped for second place by Sunderland.

Dawson, a powerful, no-nonsense centre-forward out of the old school, had learned his trade with Manchester United, along with driving right-half Nobby Lawton.

Alan Kelly was on his way to a club appearances record in the Preston goal, and full-backs George Ross, Jim Smith and centre-half Tony Singleton completed a strong and uncompromising defence.

Preston got off to a flying start with a goal after nine minutes. Holden slid the ball into the net after goalkeeper Jim Standen failed to hold a low shot from the bulldozing Dawson.

The Hammers hit back with an instant equaliser a minute later when an angled shot from Sissons out on the left made him the youngest scorer in an FA Cup final at Wembley.

It was Preston who were looking more a First Division team than West Ham, and five minutes before half-time Dawson hurled himself forward to head in a Wilson corner.

Bobby Moore, the Master, shows off the FA Cup at Wembley in 1964

There was more than a touch of good fortune about West Ham's second equaliser seven minutes into the second-half of a game that had more twists and thrills than a Hitchcock film. Geoff Hurst got his head to a corner from Peter Brabrook on the right, and the ball had just enough power behind it to roll over the line after hitting both the crossbar and goalkeeper Alan Kelly. Geoff would get another lucky bounce off that same crossbar a couple of years later!

It was only after the Hurst goal that West Ham started to unfurl the classic football for which they were to become famous in the Sixties, but the proud Preston defence refused to buckle.

Just as it seemed as if it would take extra-time to break the deadlock, old twinkle-toes Peter Brabrook made a darting run down the right and Ronnie Boyce came through the middle like a train to head in his lofted centre . Boycie kept on running and galloped around the back of the goal as Wembley erupted with cheers and choruses of Bubbles.

The winning goal had been snatched two minutes into injury time. Most neutrals thought that Preston deserved at least the reward of a replay for their contribution to a memorable match.

After skipper Bobby Moore had collected the FA Cup, 'Ticker' Boyce said: "I have scored only six goals in the League this season. Ron Greenwood had been encouraging me to come through to get on the end of crosses. It was like a dream come true to score the winning goal in a Wembley Cup final, and I think I would have run all the way out of the stadium if my team-mates had not caught up with me!'

Boycie, a product of East Ham schools football, went on to become one of West Ham's great club servants. He played 342 games in the claret and blue shirt, and later became a key member of the backroom team as a coach and then scout. He had one game in charge as caretaker manager between the going of Lou Macari and the appointment of Billy Bonds as the new boss.

Ron Greenwood said after the victory over Preston: "If you are ever going to take the lead in the match for the first time that's not a bad time to do it! But it was a bit hectic for my liking. I congratulate Preston on their magnificent performance, and we could not have grumbled if the game had gone to a replay. I am so pleased for Ronnie Boyce. I have been quietly nagging him for ages to continue his run into the box, and today he got his reward. He will go down in the West Ham history books."

*T*YPICAL – *you wait 41 years for a Wembley final and two come along at once! The Hammers were back at England's most famous football home in the spring of 1965 for a European Cup Winners' Cup final that has gone down in footballing folklore as one of the finest finals ever witnessed at Wembley. Here's our account of the match ...*

West Ham's peak performance in the Sixties came, fittingly, in front of their biggest audience, when a crammed crowd at Wembley and millions more watching on Eurvision saw them close to perfection in a memorable European Cup Winners' Cup final against Munich 1860.

Ron Greenwood selected a side showing four changes from the team that had pipped Second Division Preston in the previous season's FA Cup final. Joe Kirkup replaced the veteran John Bond at right-back, the elegant Martin Peters took Eddie Bovington's place in midfield, and virtual unknowns Alan Sealey and Brian Dear came into the attack for injured England internationals Johnny Byrne and Peter Brabrook.

Munich had eliminated favourites Torino in the semi-final, finished third in the fiercely contested Bundesliga and fielded four West German internationals. It looked an evenly balanced contest, and Greenwood told his players: "We must adopt a positive attitude. Let's go out there to win and to win in style." Across the concrete corridor separating the dressing-rooms at Wembley respected Munich coach Max Merkel was giving almost identical instructions. He, too, wanted victory in style. This in an era when more and more coaches were turning to safety-first, mass defensive methods.

West Ham fans feared that their attack would not be firing on all cylinders because of the absence of dribbling right-winger Peter Brabrook and highly skilled centre-forward 'Budgie' Byrne. But within minutes their home-produced stand-ins, Alan Sealey and Brian Dear, were making daring inroads deep into the Munich defence. Peter Radenkovic, a colourful goalkeeper from Yugoslavia, made a string of superb saves for Munich, and at the opposite end the immaculate Bobby Moore shepherded his defence into keeping composed under the pressure of swift counter-attacks. Hammers goalkeeper Jim Standen, a summertime cricketer with Worcestershire, held two magnificent catches from point-blank snap shots by Rudi Brunnenmeier, Munich's roving centre-forward and inspirational skipper.

1965 EUROPEAN CUP WINNERS'CUP FINAL

WEMBLEY STADIUM
May 19 1965

West Ham United 2, Munich 1860 0
Half-time 0-0
Scorers: Alan Sealey (2) (West Ham)
Attendance: 97,974
Referee: Istvan Zsolt (Hungary)

WEST HAM UNITED

1 Jim Standen
2 Joe Kirkup
3 Jack Burkett
4 Martin Peters
5 Ken Brown
6 Bobby Moore (captain)
7 Alan Sealey
8 Ronnie Boyce
9 Geoff Hurst
10 Brian Dear
11 John Sissons

MUNICH 1860

1 Peter Radenkovic
2 Manfred Wagner
3 Hans Reich
4 Wilfried Kohlars
5 Steven Bena
6 Otto Lutrop
7 Alfred Heiss
8 Hans Küppers
9 Rudi Brunnenmeier (capt)
10 Peter Grosser
11 Hans Rebele

Managers:
Ron Greenwood (West Ham), Max Merkel (Munich 1860)

From first kick to last, both teams produced imaginative and adventurous football and there could easily have been a shoal of goals at either end before Sealey at last made the breakthrough in the 69th minute.

It was Ronnie Boyce who set up the goal moments after the jinking John Sissons crashed a shot against a post to interrupt a tide of Munich raids. Boycie sent a defence-splitting pass arrowing through to Sealey, who instantly converted it into a goal with a low right-footed shot from 12 yards. Sealey – nicknamed Sammy – cartwheeled with delight, and just ninety seconds later had even more reason for celebration. Bobby Moore flighted a free-kick to Peters, who smartly flicked it into the goalmouth, where Sealey charged forward to force the ball over the goal-line from close range.

In the final minutes of a glorious game, Sissons again smashed a shot against the woodwork. It was sad for the gifted winger but justice for Munich, who did not deserve a three-goal defeat. They played a proud part in a classic contest.

Bobby Moore, looking as composed as if he had just been for a stroll in the park, led his team up the famous 39 steps to collect the trophy a year and 17 days after making the same journey to receive the FA Cup . He would complete an historic hat-trick in 1966.

The game would be remembered as one of the finest footballing displays ever seen at Wembley, and a lot of the credit has to go to Munich for matching West Ham's spirit of adventure. Mooro was his usual reliable and ice-cool self. West Ham and England have not had a finer servant. He was a refined defender, stamping his authority on every match and he had the gift of being able to read situations ahead of anybody else. There has rarely been a better 'big occasion' player He collected 108 caps for England, equalling Billy Wright's record of captaining the team in 90 matches. He played 545 League matches for West Ham before switching to Fulham late in his career. In his first full season at Craven Cottage he inspired Fulham to their first ever FA Cup final ... more of that in a moment.

There was a happy sequel to the Cup Winners' Cup final. Hammers and Munich shared a United Nations Fair Play Award for their sportsmanship.

Two-goal hero Alan Sealey had his career virtually finished the following year when he broke a leg falling over a bench while chasing a catch in a knockabout cricket match at the Chadwell Heath training ground. He died of a heart attack in 1996, aged 53.

Ron Greenwood was ecstatic after the victory over Munich. He said: "I am delighted for Alan who took his chances with a boldness that justified his selection. If anybody wants to know what my thinking on football is all about I would like to be judged on this match. It was close to perfection and presented the game in the best possible light. We have worked for this for four years and for us it's like reaching the summit of Everest."

Alan Sealey, two goal hero in the European Cup Winners' Cup final in 1965

*T*HE *footballing gods had fun writing the script for the 1975 FA Cup final. West Ham were back for the first time since the mid-60s, and – in an extraordinary twist – waiting for them was a Fulham team that included the greatest of all Upton Park legends, Bobby Moore. But it was not Mooro who took the headlines but an unknown lad fresh from the Fourth Division ...*

Alan Taylor started the 1974-75 season as an anonymous goal-hunter with Rochdale down in the Fourth Division. He finished as the hero of the hour for West Ham as they flattened Fulham in only the second all-London final in the 103-year history of the FA Cup. Taylor scored both goals in a 2-0 victory to add to his double strikes in the sixth round and semi-final.

Judging them on their League form, West Ham and Fulham were two unlikely finalists. West Ham had finished in the bottom half of the First Division table with only 13 victories in their 42 First Division matches, while Fulham averaged exactly one point a match in the Second Division. But, as so often happens, the FA Cup brought the best out of them. Along the road to Wembley West Ham accounted for Southampton, Swindon (after a replay), QPR, Arsenal and Ipswich; Fulham eliminated Hull, Nottingham Forest (after a third replay), Everton, Carlisle and Birmingham.

For the first time since 1952, both semi-finals went to replays before West Ham and Fulham emerged to contest a final that was peppered with personalities. Fulham featured the untouchable Mooro, who had moved to Craven Cottage fourteen months earlier. Their skipper was Alan Mullery, who had returned to his original club after eight eventful years at Tottenham.

Fulham's manager was Alec Stock, a wise old man of football who had been a showman on the soccer stage since 1949, when he was player-manager of a Yeovil Town team that shocked Sunderland (Len Shackleton and all) out of the FA Cup. He delegated the coaching duties to Bill Taylor, a shrewd tactician respected throughout football.

West Ham were skippered by one of London's most popular and competitive players in Billy Bonds and, in Trevor Brooking, they had as stylish a schemer as there was in the game. They were managed by John Lyall, an unashamed disciple of the high-principled football always practised and preached by his mentor Ron Greenwood,

THE 1975 FA CUP FINAL

WEMBLEY STADIUM,
May 3 1975

West Ham United 2, Fulham 0
Half-time 0-0
Scorer: Alan Talor 2 (West Ham)
Attendance: 100,000
Referee: Pat Partridge (Stockton-on-Tees)

WEST HAM UNITED

1 Mervyn Day
2 John McDowell
3 Frank Lampard
4 Billy Bonds (captain)
5 Tommy Taylor
6 Kevin Lock
7 Billy Jennings
8 Graham Paddon
9 Alan Taylor
10 Trevor Brooking
11 Pat Holland
12 Bobby Gould

FUHAM

1 Peter Mellor
2 John Cutbush
3 John Fraser
4 Alan Mullery (captain)
5 John Lacy
6 Bobby Moore
7 John Mitchell
8 Jim Conway
9 Viv Busby
10 Alan Slough
11 Les Barrett
12 Barry Lloyd

Managers:
John Lyall (West Ham), Alec Stock (Fulham)

Alan Taylor, two goal hero against Bobby Moore's Fulham

who had moved upstairs as general manager in charge of administration off the pitch rather than tactics on it.

A generally undistinguished game was settled in a five minute spell midway through the second-half. Alan Taylor, just twenty-one and a fine opportunist, pounced to score twice from close range after unfortunate errors by Fulham goalkeeper Peter Mellor, who had been such a reliable last line of defence all the way to Wembley.

John Lacy twice hit the woodwork, and John Mitchell had two shots well saved by nineteen-year-old goalkeeper Mervyn Day in the first hour, during which Fulham had looked the more threatening side.

Taylor's double strike killed the game stone dead, and West Ham were content to play out the rest of the game with carefully compiled possession passes.

For the first time that anybody could remember not one trainer was needed on the pitch throughout a match that was fought in a sporting spirit but without the passion usually associated with Cup finals.

Mullery and Mooro walked off at the end with their arms around each other, looking around the Wembley Stadium one last time as if they both knew this was their swansong at the ground both had graced with exceptional performances.

"We had a plan to stifle West Ham in midfield and attack them at the heart of their defence," said Alec Stock. "But it didn't work and by the time we were thinking of switching to Plan B the young lad Taylor broke us with his two well-taken goals. I am not going to say anything negative about our goalkeeper. He has been outstanding all season, and the ball just did not run kindly for him today. I thought Mullery and Moore conducted themselves with great dignity. Both have been wonderful ambassadors for football in general and, recently, Fulham."

An almost numb with disbelief Alan Taylor said: "I can't help thinking that this is all a dream. It seems like only yesterday that I was playing with Rochdale in front of 3,000 supporters."

Injuries restricted Alan's appearances to 98 League matches and 25 goals. He later played for Norwich, Cambridge United, Vancouver Whitecaps, Hull, Burnley and Bury before finishing back at Norwich, where he later ran a newsagents business.

Mooro commented after his rare defeat at Wembley: "I will always have claret and blue blood, and I'm delightd West Ham have won the Cup again. But I would have been much happier if it had been Fulham!

PUBLISHER **Terry Baker** writes: "All of us at A1 Sporting Books are fanatics about sports facts and figures, and we like to lay out our stats so that they are easy to read and not set in a tiny type that challenges the eyesight. Our resident statistician **Michael Giller** provides the following facts feast for West Hammers. Enjoy ..."

ALL-TIME ROLL OF HONOUR

Football League best position
3rd place 1985-86 'Old' First Division
'Old' Second Division Champions:
1957-58, 1980-81
Championship Play-off Winners
2004-05
FA Cup Winners
1963-64, 1974-75, 1979-80
FA Cup Runners-up
1922-23, 2005-06
European Cup Winners' Cup Winners
1964-65
European Cup Winners' Cup Runners-up
1975-76
League Cup Finalists
1965-66, 1980-81
Intertoto Cup Winners
1998-99
Football League War Cup Winners
1940
FA Premier Academy U19 Champions
1998-99, 1999-2000
FA Youth Cup Winners
1963, 1981, 1999
South-East Counties Champions
1984-85, 1995-96, 1997-98

West Ham's main objective at the start of the 1979-80 season was promotion, but the closest they came to challenging the leaders was fifth place in March. They finally finished seventh.

The West Ham goalscorers in the League that season – amassing 54 goals between them – were:

David Cross 13, Ray Stewart 10 (7 pens), Alan Devonshire 5, Stuart Pearson 5, Pat Holland 4, Geoff Pike 4, Trevor Brooking 3, Paul Allen 2, Alvin Martin 2, Billy Bonds 1, Billy Lansdowne 1, Nicky Morgan 1, Jimmy Neighbour 1, 2 own goals

The 13 goals scored in the FA Cup came from: Ray Stewart 3 (2 pens), Trevor Brooking 2, Stuart Pearson 2, Geoff Pike, Paul Allen, David Cross, Alan Devonshire, Frank Lampard, 1 own goal

SECOND DIVISION TABLE 1979-80

		P	W	D	L	F	A	Pts
1	Leicester City	42	21	13	8	58	38	55
2	Sunderland	42	21	12	9	69	42	54
3	Birmingham City	42	21	11	10	58	38	53
4	Chelsea	42	23	7	12	66	52	53
5	QPR	42	18	13	11	75	53	49
6	Luton Town	42	16	17	9	66	45	49
7	*West Ham United*	*42*	*20*	*7*	*15*	*54*	*43*	*47*
8	Cambridge United	42	14	16	12	61	53	44
9	Newcastle United	42	15	14	13	53	49	44
10	Preston North End	42	12	19	11	56	52	43
11	Oldham Athletic	42	16	11	15	49	53	43
12	Swansea City	42	17	9	16	48	53	43
13	Shrewsbury Town	42	18	5	19	60	53	41
14	Orient	42	12	17	13	48	54	41
15	Cardiff City	42	16	8	18	41	48	40
16	Wrexham	42	16	6	20	40	49	38
17	Notts County	42	11	15	16	51	52	37
18	Watford	42	12	13	17	39	46	37
19	Bristol Rovers	42	11	13	18	50	64	35
20	Fulham	42	11	7	24	42	74	29
21	Burnley	42	6	15	21	39	73	27
22	Charlton Athletic	42	6	10	26	39	78	22

LEAGUE CUP CHALLENGERS

The Hammers also made a strong challenge for the Football League Cup in the eventful 1979-80 season. They eliminated Barnsley, Southend and Sunderland before going out to Brian Clough's European Cup holders Nottingham Forest in the fifth round. losing 3-0 in extra-time in a replay after a goalless draw at Upton Park. West Ham scored 14 goals in the League Cup: David Cross 5, Billy Lansdowne 3, Trevor Brooking, Stuart Pearson, Pat Holland, Ray Stewart (pen), Geoff Pike and Alvin Martin.

The following season, the Irons went close to a Double when they won the Second Division title and finished runners-up in the League Cup final to League champions Liverpool. They drew 1-1 at Wembley on Match 14 1981 after extra-time, Alan Kennedy scoring for Liverpool and Ray Stewart equalising from the spot to force a replay. In the replay at Villa Park on Wednesday April 1 Liverpool won 2-1 with goals from Alan Hansen and Kenny Dalglish. Paul Goddard scoring West Ham's goal.

West Ham have had 19 club captains since the Second World War. Bobby Moore had the longest run, 13 years. Billy Bonds, the only Hammers captain to lift the FA Cup twice, had an 11 year run. This it the captains' table:

Charles Bicknell (1945-47)

Dick Walker (1947-51

Malcolm Allison (1951-57)

Noel Cantwell (1957-60)

Ken Brown (1960-61)

Bobby Moore (1961-74)

Billy Bonds (1974-84)

Alvin Martin (1984-90)

Ian Bishop (1990-92)

Julian Dicks (1992-93)

Steve Potts (1993-96)

Julian Dicks (1996-97)

Steve Lomas (1997-01)

Paolo Di Canio (2001-03)

Joe Cole (2003)

Christian Dailly (2003-05)

Nigel Reo-Coker (2005-07)

Lucas Neill (2007-09)

Matthew Upson (2009-)

Cork-born Noel Cantwell was the first non-British captain. Three years after leaving the Hammers he collected the FA Cup as skipper of Manchester United at Wembley in 1963.

EXTRA-TIME: Appearances and Scorers

TOP TEN APPEARANCES

793 Billy Bonds (1967–88)
674 Frank Lampard Sr. (1967–85)
646 Bobby Moore (1958–74)
635 Trevor Brooking (1967–84)
601 Alvin Martin (1977–96)
548 Jimmy Ruffell (1921–37)
506 Steve Potts (1985–2002)
505 Vic Watson (1920–35)
502 Geoff Hurst (1959–72)
467 Jim Barrett (1924–43)

TOP TEN GOAL SCORERS

326 Vic Watson (1920–35)
252 Geoff Hurst (1959–72)
166 John Dick (1953–63)
166 Jimmy Ruffell (1921–37)
146 Tony Cottee (1983–88), (94–96)
107 Johnny Byrne (1961–67)
104 Bryan Robson (1970–74), (76–79)
102 Trevor Brooking (1967–84)
100 Malcolm Musgrove (1953–63)
100 Martin Peters (1962–70)

Most League Goals In A Season
101, Division Two (1957–58)

Top League Scorer In A Season:
Vic Watson (42) (Div 1 1929–30)

Top All Goals Scorer In A Season
Vic Watson (50) (Div 1 1929–30)

Most Goals In One Match
Vic Watson 6
v Leeds United (h) 1929
Geoff Hurst (right)
v Sunderland (h) 1968

Brian Dear 5 in 20 minutes
v West Brom (h) 1965

Art Turner 2010

Norman Giller was a sports reporter for the Stratford Express when the paper helped launch the Hammer of the Year poll in West Ham's promotion year of 1958 in conjunction with the West Ham Supporters' Club. Scott Parker (below) was the 33rd player to have his name on the coveted trophy.

2009-10 SCOTT PARKER
2008-09 SCOTT PARKER
2007-08 ROBERT GREEN
2006-07 CARLOS TEVEZ
2005-06 DANNY GABBIDON
2004-05 TEDDY SHERINGHAM
2003-04 MATTHEW ETHERINGTON
2002-03 JOE COLE
2001-02 SEBASTIEN SCHEMMEL
2000-01 STUART PEARCE
1999-00 PAOLO DI CANIO
1998-99 SHAKA HISLOP
1997-98 RIO FERDINAND
1996-97 JULIAN DICKS
1995-96 JULIAN DICKS
1994-95 STEVE POTTS
1993-94 TREVOR MORLEY
1992-93 STEVE POTTS
1991-92 JULIAN DICKS
1990-91 LUDEK MIKLOSKO
1989-90 JULIAN DICKS
1988-89 PAUL INCE
1987-88 STEWART ROBSON
1986-87 BILLY BONDS
1985-86 TONY COTTEE
1984-85 PAUL ALLEN
1983-84 TREVOR BROOKING
1982-83 ALVIN MARTIN
1981-82 ALVIN MARTIN
1980-81 PHIL PARKES
1979-80 ALVIN MARTIN
1978-79 ALAN DEVONSHIRE
1977-78 TREVOR BROOKING
1976-77 TREVOR BROOKING
1975-76 TREVOR BROOKING

Art Turner 2010

1974-75 BILLY BONDS
1973-74 BILLY BONDS
1972-73 BRYAN ROBSON
1971-72 TREVOR BROOKING
1970-71 BILLY BONDS
1969-70 BOBBY MOORE
1968-69 GEOFF HURST
1967-68 BOBBY MOORE
1966-67 GEOFF HURST
1965-66 GEOFF HURST
1964-65 MARTIN PETERS
1963-64 JOHNNY BYRNE
1962-63 BOBBY MOORE
1961-62 LAWRIE LESLIE
1960-61 BOBBY MOORE
1959-60 MALCOLM MUSGROVE
1958-59 KEN BROWN
1957-58 ANDY MALCOLM